EATING THE ASHES

EATING THE ASHES

SEEKING
REHABILITATION
WITHIN THE US PENAL SYSTEM

Veronica Compton-Wallace

Algora Publishing
New York

Library of Congress Cataloging-in-Publication Data

Compton, Veronica.
  Eating the ashes : seeking rehabilitation within the US penal system /
Veronica Compton.
    p. cm.
  ISBN 0-87586-164-4 (softcover) — ISBN 0-87586-165-2 (hardcover)
  1. Women prisoners—United States. 2. Women
Prisoners—Rehabilitation—United States. I. Title.

HV9471 .C657 2002
365'.43—dc21

                          2002014689

Front Cover: Drawing by Veronica Compton, State Penitentiary, 1985

Printed in the United States

I am like a pelican of the wilderness: I am like an owl of the desert. I watch, and am as a sparrow alone upon the housetop. Mine enemies reproach me all the day; and they that are mad against me are sworn against me. For I have eaten ashes like bread, and mingled my drink with weeping.

Psalms 102: 6-9

This book is dedicated to the inmates and staff who have worked so tirelessly to bring about positive change and improvement in the US prison system. It is especially gratifying to know that the most recent Administration at WCCW is deeply dedicated to promoting a positive atmosphere for rehabilitation, to advancing and expanding the sort of programs we participated in. Their willingness to enlist inmates in real and responsible joint efforts is a very bright spot in the dark world of incarceration. No one knows how far this light will reach, how much difference it will make; but it brings hope: bread for the eaters of ashes.

TABLE of CONTENTS

Preface	1
Foreword	5
1. First Realization — "The Ashes"	9
2. Background of the Study: An Inside View of Corrections	17
Some Facts about Women and Violent Crimes	20
Signs of Trouble are Many	21
Cruel and Unusual Punishment Instead of Mental Health Care	35
The Prison Clinic	35
3. Diagnostic Dilemmas in Psychological Assessments	41
4. Data Collection and Evaluation — Pitfalls and Success Strategies	51
Quantitative Data	52
Qualitative Data	53
Data Used in this Study	58
5. POCAAN and Peer Education	61
Effective Programs in Correctional Education — Applying the Principles in Practice	61
Implementing POCAAN	63
The Special Needs Unit	65
6. The Alternatives To Violence Program (AVP) and Peace Talks	69
The Opening Talk	73
The Eight Main Sessions	77
Lectures	84
Structure of Lecture Sessions	86
7. Trouble in TEC	89
Power over Our Own Life	89
Results of Powerless in Prison	93
In TEC: An Extreme Environment	95
A Step in the Right Direction	96

8. The Effects of Abuse   101
    Post-Traumatic Stress Disorder   101
    Recognizing Abuse: The Victim's Awareness Manual   107
    Voices of the Innocent   110

9. TEC and the Beginnings of Betterment   113
    Expanding with Volunteers   118
    Expanding the Range of Activities   120
    Program Coordinator Duties   122

10. Inmates' and Families' Needs   125
    Case Study — TEC Resident Annie   126
    Case Study — TEC Resident Barbie   128
    The Parenting Instructor's View   130
    A Community Leader's View   134
    The Children Left Behind   136

11. The Survey   139
    The Questionnaire and Representative Responses   142
    Voices of the Inmates   156

12. Recommendations   169
    Educational Design   169
    Two Steps Forward, One Step Back   172
    The View from WCCW's Education Department   172
    Thoughts for the Future   174

13. Conclusion   179

Appendixes   188

Resources   203

Acknowledgements   207

PREFACE

A growing number of writers are presenting the voices of incarcerated females. What is unique in Veronica Compton Wallace's work is the fact that she is the ultimate insider, as a long-term inmate herself. There is no danger of her "going native"; she *is*. There are truths shared by her fellow inmates and friends that might never be exposed to a researcher wearing a "visitor's" badge. She can tell us not only what a cell in "the hole" looks like, but what it feels like to call that isolation unit home for six months. She has witnessed and felt both the violence and the caring that occur 24-7 inside the wire. She knows what happens and doesn't happen after lights out. She knows where things have been hidden and how it's done. She learned first to survive, and then to lead in this mini-society that most people would rather not acknowledge. Veronica Compton Wallace did not arrive at The Washington Corrections Center for Women as a model prisoner by any means. Over the years, a transformation has occurred which has taken her from angry rebel to a tireless campaigner, teacher, and worker for her fellow inmates. This book tells her story and theirs.

The reader will do well to keep in mind that one inmate's perspective of a condition or an event does not always account for the big picture in a large institution. At any given time, numerous scenarios and dynamics are being played out which may give the impression, to an individual who feels put upon anyway, that her situation is unjust and out of control, when in fact it is the result of institutional priorities.

1

The programs and activities Veronica describes that assisted in her rehabilitation are constantly under fire, and are often portrayed as "draining scarce resources" or being too "soft on crime" and criminals. The fact is that women by and large respond to constructive programs. The return on investment for a rehabilitated ex-felon far outweighs the cost of programs that produce change.

We can logically assume that societies have always struggled with the concept of crime, the motivation to commit criminal acts, and the punishments and treatment of convicted individuals. The history of this struggle is rich, often shocking and repulsive, and even humorous. Concluding that the struggle existed long before mankind began to write about it does not present much of an intellectual challenge.

The definition of a "crime" is influenced by the variables of culture, time, degree and gender. Murder and rape are considered far more justifiable in some societies than others. Substance abuse is tolerated in some European countries to a much greater degree than in the United States. There was a time when trafficking in human beings, or in mind-altering drugs, was not considered a criminal act, but petty thievery might land an "offender" in a distant penal colony to serve a long sentence under the harshest conditions. Even more absurd are many of the "reasons" (crimes) for which women have historically been convicted, among them promiscuity, adultery, and failure to obey husbands! It is intriguing to contemplate what acts our prehistoric ancestors might have considered acceptable versus those things that were regarded as crimes against the society.

Those who contemplate human nature and motivation search for "reasons why." Early childhood development theories, strain, social bonding, social learning theories, and mental illness are all considered factors in "why" the criminal deliberately commits acts that are harmful to the individual and general good. Critical theorists might argue that oppression and socio-economic factors are largely to blame for criminal activities. Joanne Belknap argues in her book *The Invisible Woman* that if socio-economic factors drive men to commit crimes, then women are to be commended for their relatively low rate of crime in light of the fact that they experience even more pressure than men do.

WCCW now takes in some 1000 new admissions per year; 85% of them test below 9th-grade level for basic skills (reading, writing, and math). Fully 50% of that group is performing below the 5th-grade level. Washington State law requires those below 9th grade to be enrolled in school, but provides no post-secondary opportunities to incarcerated persons. Until 1995, Washington inmates could take lower level college courses offered at prison sites through the community colleges. A two-year Associate Degree in technology (vocational)

2

was also available. Although the demand for post secondary education is not great among inmates, there are still some who look beyond the GED and minimal job skills training now offered.

In the fall of 1999, I gathered 37 interested female inmates to explore avenues for education beyond those offered by my department at Washington Corrections Center for Women. Veronica Compton was the only attendee who had "outside" funding, and enough college-level credits to qualify for a bachelor's degree completion program offered by The Evergreen State College. Two years later, in June of 2002, representatives from Evergreen attended our annual graduation and awards ceremony to present Veronica the degree of Bachelor of Science in Human Studies. Much of the information presented in this book was generated during or was used as a part of her course of studies. Other parts come from a detailed and copious diary that she has maintained for many years.

In this book Veronica goes beyond the crime and considers the programs and services that might bring about behavioral change. Specifically, she makes a case for different thinking between the way men are incarcerated and the way women "do time." She calls on her experience as a long-term inmate to explore the "punishment and treatment" of women offenders. Only recently, as the number of incarcerated women has risen drastically, have we begun to get serious about changing the male model of prison. The potential returns to taxpayers and most certainly the saving of lives and human dignity in the rehabilitated female felon dictate that we continue to change the current model.

Larry Richardson
Education Director
The Washington Corrections Center for Women

Foreword

This study is not meant to excuse or diminish the culpability of any woman incarcerated at WCCW, myself included. All of us in here are in varying degrees aware of the burden of guilt each carries for what she has done and many have spent countless nights for years as I have, reflecting on how our actions have hurt innocent lives. Every crime affects not just the victim, but family, friends, and even the sense of security of the community. Recognizing our accountability for this is the first step toward a genuine rehabilitation. We have to take personal responsibility for our actions, but a major part of a genuine rehabilitation is recognition of what led us to do what we did. I hope this book will be of direct help to the many women I know who feel genuine remorse but feel trapped in a revolving door of crime and incarceration. I also hope it may be of help to society to make the best use of the incarceration process to prevent recidivism.[1]

To prevent crime it is necessary to understand what leads an individual to commit a crime. The commonsense view of this, especially with respect to women, is that what leads women to commit crimes or stay with abusive men who are both dangerous and criminal is that the woman has chosen crime, much as one might choose a particular make of automobile. If any motive is assigned, it usually runs no deeper than to say they are crazy. The craziness of women rises

---

1. All author's profits from this printing of this book will be donated to charities: Washington State Children Victims of Crime, and Rebuilding Families Program, WCCW

to a spectacular pitch when one considers that the great majority of female felons have been involved with an abusive, violent male for a large part of their lives. The commonsense question is, of course, why don't they run away? And even worse, if they do leave, why do they immediately connect with another one who is just the same? The presumption is that when threatened, we either fight or flee. Indeed, scientific study (of male subjects) has suggested that that's just what people actually do. If so, then female behavior would indeed appear to be just a choice — they must want to stay with the abuse and commit crimes. However, in 2000, this view received a serious shock.

At UCLA, a team of women researchers decided to see what actual brain chemistry as well as behavior might be created in women when they were subjected to stress.[2] They discovered that there was a major difference in female brain chemistry. Where males responded with a burst of adrenaline and other "fight or flight" chemicals, the females added oxytocin, a calming element. This led them to prefer bonding with other women and their children, rather than the male response of belligerence or retreat. The women's actual conduct tended to confirm the effect of the oxytocin.

At first blush, though this experiment did show a bonding tendency under stress, it appears to suggest that it would lead women away from, rather than toward, their abusers. However, there is a major difference between stress induced in a lab setting on volunteers and that involved in domestic violence. To see what happens to the bonding impulse in situations of real threat of death or great bodily harm, we can consider the Stockholm Syndrome.

The Stockholm Syndrome takes its name from a situation in a Stockholm bank some years ago where robbers took the employees hostage and threatened to kill them if their demands were not met. In this impossible situation, the women employees bonded intensely to their captors, to such an extent that even when the siege ended, they regarded the police as their enemies and the robbers as their defenders. Significantly, *the women bonded only with the male robbers, not with each other*. This phenomenon is now so common in an age of hostage taking that it is a recognized psychological reaction and one which is far more common among female hostages than male. To explain the switch from bonding with the innocent and bonding with the abuser, one need only consider the difference between the relatively innocuous stress of a lab and the terror atmosphere of hostage taking. John Stuart Mill once remarked that differences in degree can easily become differences in kind. This appears to be a case of differences in

---

2. Taylor, S.E.,Klein,L.C., Lewis, B.P., Gruenewald, T.L., Gurung,R.A.R. and Updegraff, J.A.:"Female Responses to Stress: Tend and Befriend, Not Fight or Flight." <u>Psychological Review</u>, (2000) 107, (3), PP.41-429.

degree of threat amounting to differences in kind of response. And all this rests heavily on brain chemistry, not on conscious choices.

Another element acting below the level of full consciousness is Post Traumatic Syndrome. One of the startling things we found among the women at WCCW was that more than 90% of them had suffered serious abuse. Most of it involved violence, sexuality, extreme brutality and mortal threat. The result of trauma of this sort is that it often primes the individual to revisit the trauma on very slight stimulus. In such a situation the person will seek to appease, even at the price of committing dangerous or criminal actions; and even though the aggressor has done only a little — that "little" amounts to a major threat to the victim. By such means the cunning manipulator can secure what appears to be the willing compliance of the PTSD sufferer.

I believe that the path to prevention of recidivism, for many (though not all) women, lies in discovering the roots of their frailty and at last being able to cope with their demons and emerge into the light of true choice. This book is dedicated to helping them, and others who wish to put an end to crime, to see what can be done.

1. First Realization — "The Ashes"

I'm a woman who was found guilty of attempting the most serious of crimes — murder. This book deals with what I found and learned in an experience that few women have ever had, and none has ever written about in much detail. In my twenty-plus years as a prisoner, I have been afforded a rare view of correctional evolution. Having experienced some of the best and worst of penal design and theory, I've chosen to highlight what I've found to prove successful; success being measured in human emotional healing and cognitive well being, the combination making for what we think of as rehabilitation.

When I came down off drugs, in prison, and began to realize what I had tried to do, I had two choices — to deny or rationalize in an attempt to cover up my fear of reality, or to try to find that unknown which had led me there. I chose the latter. To find the answer, I had to take a gut wrenching inventory of my soul. Reading in sociology and psychology added value, but as the unknown was beginning to take shape, I was to discover I was not alone in my misconceptions.

At first, I considered myself to be out of place. I didn't belong there, in that crowd of dangerous criminals. Someone had made some sort of mistake. I didn't know why, but I thought the others were truly deviant; not just individuals who had made a crazy mistake. So I tried to evoke my toughest façade, as a way of protecting the person I really was inside. In the meantime, to maintain avoidance of reality and responsibility I found ways to get drugs to take me away from "the horror of it all." I expected that the prison system would recognize what was wrong with me and set it right. Wasn't that "rehabilitation," after all? Back in the 1980s, fragments of programs designed earlier to achieve the rehabilitation of the prisoners remained, though many program titles now served only to cover the institution's two major objectives: retribution and control, with emphasis on the latter.

During the early 1980s, Washington State was weaning itself from the 1960-70s rehabilitation model. Dubbed the "model prison" in the United States in the 1970s, by 1980 Purdy Treatment Center for Women had begun to lose its luster. The traces left were behavior-modification practices which — given the political temperament of the day — were forced to get in synch with the new pendulum swing of a punishment theory. The prison's name was changed to establish the beginning of this hard-edged new era: Washington Correctional Center for Women.

Unknowingly, I was a participant in these new corrections-minded punishment theories (adverse behavior modification). Gone were the once open discussions between staff and prisoners. Attempts to educate the women received less and less funding. Everything was changing and the prison was a chaotic hodge-podge of theories and practice. The newly embraced "punish them and throw away the key" was here, as was the separation into an "us" and "them." This fueled an enormously limited view of who female criminals were and what their impact was on society. Negative assertions ran out of control, like a runaway train.

Crimiphobia was born. Behavioral modification practices were distorted. While many remnants of this still remain and may (when utilized correctly) assist in establishing desirable behaviors, they do have a flip side. When the state agencies implement such concepts, the actual practitioners who supply the incentives or remove them are not trained or competent to render such judgment calls. The results I've witnessed hastened or perhaps even pushed some women to commit suicide, or to self-mutilate, and emotionally break down, becoming fragments of who they previously had been.

I discovered that the main function of the prison psychologists was to come up with a diagnosis and prescriptions for treatment as part of the prisoner's identity profile. If the label attached to the inmate was negative, it would affect her chances of parole (something that still existed in the system, at that time). Not only did the psychologist freely diagnose us on the basis of unsubstantiated pre-sentencing reports prepared by zealous and cynical prosecuting attorneys, they regularly assigned terms which carried the unspoken but understood tag: "untreatable." Worst of all, once such a note went into a woman's file, it remained there, even though subsequent diagnoses might be contradictory. No one ever tried to establish the accuracy of anything in the file; by its mere existence, it became fact.

I was initially diagnosed as having bipolar personality disorder, when factually it was behavior associated with the withdrawal from my heavy cocaine use. Later the diagnosis was amplified to "schizophrenic with paranoid aspects", again drug abuse induced, rather than a longstanding mental disorder. When Administration became aware of my drug use but was unable to catch me at it, the additional terms "devious and manipulative" were added to my "profile."

At first, I assumed that the psychological services were there as a part of the healing mission of medicine, but I soon found that all too often they were simply part of the control apparatus of the prison. Rather than treat underlying psychological conditions, they frequently prescribed drugs to diminish symptoms and actions which created control problems. "Downers," Lithium, and as a last resort, the dreaded Special Needs Unit, a place where women were controlled by extreme punishment, if all else had failed.

In my case, the "counselor" to whom I naively poured out the trouble I was having with another inmate cunningly suggested they could not move me to another cell unless I agreed that I could not control my hatred of the other woman. When I accepted the offer, a panel was convened and their recommendation was that I be moved, to Administrative Segregation, also known as the "Hole."

During my off and on years in isolation, I witnessed the twists and turns of policy, of methodology and control. Here the behavioral reward and punishment (deprivation) system was in its exploratory form. Conditions were very extreme during the early 1980s; gradually, improvements came and some went, then returned by the late 1990s.

AD SEG is meant to control. Isolation and various deprivations there are mostly last resort forms of sanctioning a prisoner who defies the rules. Then, too, on occasion, a woman is held in what is termed "investigation."

The years I lived in AD SEG have long since passed, but the isolation experiences remain some of the best and worst of times in my life. I managed to survive where many fell apart and became babbling children, or worse: cruel, sadistic animals. There were suicides. There were suicide attempts and self-mutilations. There were perversions and expressions of mental illness (psychotic-episodes), and there were heroic acts of courage, kindness and compassion. What I have borne witness to has led me to conduct the study you are about to read.

While I was in the Hole, I was befriended by another inmate who undertook to cure me of my drug addiction. Under her guidance, I began to learn the second and most important lesson: that we prisoners, no matter what we had done, were real persons, not monsters. As with the first lesson, at first I only applied it to myself; it would take time for the full meaning to sink in.

Shortly after leaving the Hole, I was accepted in one of the remaining enlightened programs in the system, called STOP. It aimed to identify both the causes and the symptoms of drug addiction in such a way that the woman could understand what she was doing to herself. The program was run by a combination of concerned professional outsiders and reformed drug users. Since their aim was cure, not control, they looked carefully at the prisoner's history rather than routinely repeating the reports in the files. In my case, they recognized that my behavior was actually due to an erratic supply of drugs. Now that I had given them up, there wasn't anything in my behavior that looked "bipolar" anymore. Also, since my experience had been part of the 1980s cocaine epidemic in the Hollywood area, they concluded that my crime was a result of "drug induced psychosis." For the first time, I was returned to the world of the sane.

This lesson taught me two things. The first was that actual help by others with experience could achieve results that the control-oriented theories did not. The second was that those who had actually been through something like heavy drug use could be of the greatest help in dealing with symptoms that inexperienced outsiders could so neatly mislabel.

Experience with genuinely helpful professionals moderated my cynical rejection of the whole business of mental health, but after what I had gone through with their predecessors, I approached this team with much greater care. I learned that one very good clue to what they really meant to do lay in the amount of time they would spend talking to me, rather than reading reports. The control types just processed us; they already knew what we were. Not only did I finally find that I was getting help, for the first time I felt the stirrings of a desire to be helpful to others.

By then, I had been in prison for more than six years and, given how many women had come and gone, the younger ones liked to call me "Mom." In 1985, I created Outreach, a prison-run program to bring women from "general population" into contact with the "problem cases" in the Special Needs Unit. It was simple and direct. We went in and talked to them, but more important, we learned to listen. Since we were just about the only people in their lives that weren't telling them what to do, and threatening or carrying out threats, they opened up to us. One older lady was so delusional she thought she was the Queen of Denmark. Even so, she was perceptive enough to imagine me as Annette Funicello — someone I did resemble. The greatest benefit I got from the experience was to realize that even presumably crazy people can be helped. What they needed most was for someone to reach out to them and listen. Inside their obsessional ravings was a kernel of experience and a cry for real help.

The program that brought us in was a start, but it couldn't go very far beyond our listening. No one listened to us any more than to them; the overriding issue for Administration was quiet security, not the mental health of the women in Special Needs.

In the next two years, I served on the Inmate Council, an administrative platform where we were heard — as long as it served their purposes. At the same time, there was an accelerated building program aimed at increased security. In the 1980s, the place had resembled a college campus, but as time passed it began to look like a prison camp. Fences, razor wire, internal cross fencing, cheap housing for an expanded population, and ever tighter measures of control, deprivation and segregation of various degrees of offenders all took place in what seemed (given the relative peacefulness of the place) an incomprehensible obsession with security. When an outside visitor with some experience of prisons remarked that the place now resembled a standard men's penitentiary, I realized what had happened. The theory and practice of the Department of Corrections was now completely dominated by the idea that women prisoners differed from men only in their physical sex characteristics. Understanding and rehabilitation had been scrapped; control and retribution now drove policy.

Outside forces that were driving the situation in this negative way also worked for us, sometimes. Drugs and the AIDS epidemic spurred the creation of independent groups whose concerns led them to approach government with offers of help. Prison populations were statistical standouts in these problem areas. In 1992, the People of Color Against Aids Network approached the prison with an offer to engage in an educational program for prisoners. They recognized that it would be more effective to reach the women inside by recruiting inmates to present basic information on sexuality and safe or, anyway, safer practices. I saw an opportunity, and for six years gave basic orientation for them to every entering prisoner, which numbered in the hundreds. The inmates' reaction was a revelation. Instead of being bored or resentful, they were almost pathetically eager to learn more. My presentations were earthy but the information was reliable — POCAAN made sure of that, and so did I. It was then that I began to realize that my childhood dream of being a researcher was emerging.

I was fortunate to be a guest speaker in lectures for the chemical dependency program, and relished the opportunity to work with high-risk inmates as well. If information/education could help save one mother, the work was worth the effort. It was clear to administrators that many women who exhibited high-risk behaviors also exhibited a pattern of chronic bad choices in life. I spoke on self-esteem, domestic violence, "HIV 101," and other related topics.

Then, in 1996, there was a chance to move beyond sex and drugs to what I was just beginning to recognize as a root problem: violence. Part of my work for POCAAN had been to collect responses to a questionnaire they furnished. One of the questions dealt with abuse. The response was overwhelming.

The comments the women had written in made it clear that a majority had experienced violence, often coupled with sexual abuse. Now, the Administration agreed to embrace the Quaker program called Alternatives to Violence. Administration hoped it would diminish the unruliness and petty violence between inmates. I saw it in a larger context: coping with the generational cycles of dependency and abuse.

From 1996 to 2000, I was a Facilitator in the Alternatives to Violence program, which led me to the issue of post-traumatic stress syndrome and the paradoxical finding that the victims of violence may become violent themselves, and often seek out violent partners for further abuse. I became interested in psychological and neurological research work that had been done, knowing that as long as the evidence was simply behavioral, critics would claim the syndrome didn't exist and was merely an excuse for bad behavior.

By 1998, I was ready to try applying what I'd learned, in the TEC Unit (the renamed SNU). Conditions there were severe. Women were sometimes pepper sprayed, or threatened or punished with "five points" — spread-eagled leather-belt restraining on a table/bed) and only the most minimal civilized amenities. When lawsuits on behalf of these women finally rattled Administration, a more humane and enlightened staff was put into place. I offered proposals for programs aimed at resurrecting the humanity of these brutalized women, which were accepted.

The TEC Betterment Program was born. Our whole aim was to deal with the consequences of what, often, had been an entire lifetime of abuse for these women. The goal of the Betterment program was to provide avenues for self-expression through art, music, poetry, writing and reading, crafts, and personal assistance projects. Allowing inmates to have creative expression as well as receive personal attention in approaching other arenas of their lives was significantly successful. All of this was only possible because of the close cooperation between the humane staff members and our team of volunteers. I was in charge of this from 1998 to 2000.

As my date for possible parole came near, I tried to recruit people to take over all the various programs when I left. Whether I have the opportunity to return to my family or continue where I am, I remain deeply interested in the relationship between sustained abuse and crime, and I plan to go on researching and working in these areas.

I can't believe anyone is capable of remedying a thing until they first recognize there's something wrong. Because I am on the inside and have undergone this experience, I am granted a rare opportunity to report in greater depth and degree than any other female reporter heretofore. In this book I offer the insights I have gained into the special situation of women in prison. Also suggested are the kinds of programs that enable these women to develop that humanity which was taken from them — or, in many cases, was denied to them — in their "pre-crime" lives.

I will present excerpts from my study, and offer the words of many women who are using the shock landing in prison to spur fundamental, positive changes in their lives. Principally, I will share firsthand testimony to success and failure, benefit and detriment, and ultimately the good derived from these programs, which have succeeded in their aims.

As in all social progress, groundbreaking must occur before new roads may be paved. It is my hope that this work will inspire other women to help build these roads.

2. Background of the Study: An Inside View of Corrections

In 1981, I began experiencing life inside of Washington State's Women's Prison. This journey has continued for over two decades and has taken me into the offices of correctional officials, attorneys, and psychiatrists, into courtrooms, segregation cells, the prison mental wards and dayrooms. As I explore this peculiar environment, real-life interviews with individuals in every role have aided me in my work and have provided a thorough and comprehensive view of the system of corrections now being implemented at what is formally known as the Washington Correctional Center for Women (WCCW).

As an incarcerated felon with a very long sentence, I have had the opportunity to know and talk with women who had been incarcerated before "my time" as well as those who came in during my time at WCCW. Prisoners are social creatures, for the most part, and they talk freely about many aspects of their lives. They often told me things they would prudently conceal from prison staff. As I exposed details of my history, they felt free to do so as well. Trust developed and grew bit by bit as we exchanged confidences. As long as I was willing to give it "up front" first, intimate details of other women's lives were laid out for me.

Over the years I came to see that, although the formal structure of WCCW is supposed to be the same as that of the men's institutions, in fact there was a false equality of treatment. It was false because the female felon experiences the deprivations of incarceration differently than men do; but, more seriously, because the motives and causes of her criminal activity seem so different from those of males. Indeed, as I came to see, her basic psychology is different.

The Equal Protection Clause of the United States Constitution requires more of a state law than a non-discriminatory application within the class it establishes.... It imposes a requirement of some rationality in the nature of the class singled out. To be sure, the constitutional demand is not a demand that a statute necessarily apply equally to all persons. The Constitution does not require things which are different in fact to be treated in the law as though they were the same.

Tigger v. Texas 310 US 141 1940):
Rinaldi v. Yeager US 305 1960)

The Equal Protection Clause requires the consideration of whether the classifications drawn by any statute constitute an arbitrary and invidious discrimination.

The statute will be upheld where gender classification is not invidious, but rather reflects the fact that the sexes are not similarly situated in certain circumstances. 404 US 71 1971.

The present system for the processing of male offenders cannot serve as a model for the processing of female offenders, nor should the male-focused data offered be considered representative of female inmates' needs or situations.

It is important to understand that this book intentionally speaks in terms of female arrestees. Almost all of the implemented studies that have been done on incarceration have focused on male felons, and the conclusions derived have been applied to the female population without any consideration of differences. My experience has led me to think that the conclusions might not be applicable across the gender divide; that the whole penal system has based its approach on an assumption of similarity that is false.

As for the gravity of the problem, the data are telling. (Note that statistical variances are due to different sources.):

- In 1998, an estimated total of 3.2 million arrests were made in the U.S.; 22% were women.
- As of the year 2000, women were 5% of the state prison population nationally. In Washington State, women account for 7.3%.
- Nationally, state inmates serve an average of 5½ years on a 10-year sentence. In Washington State, 28.3% of women in prison will serve in

excess of ten years (violent offenders are allowed a 50% reduction in sentence, at most).

- Based on self-reports of victims of violence, women account for 14% of violent offenders.
- State prison populations contain on average 2.1 million violent offenders. National statistics reflect that women average just 8% of all those convicted for violent offenses, 23% of property offenses, and 17% of drug offenses.
- In 1998, more than 750,000 women were under correctional supervision, about 1% of the U.S. female population.
- Washington Correctional Center for Women is Washington State's only prison for female felons and currently houses 900+ women, all sentenced in excess of 1 year and 1 day.

Offense Category	
Murder (1 + 2 degree)	12.5%
Manslaughter	1.7%
Sex Crimes	10.3%
Robbery	10.3%
Assault	17.5%
Property Crimes	14.8%
Drug Crimes	21.5%

The National Center on Addiction and Substance Abuses at Columbia University gave the statistic that 80% of state prisoners had substance abuse problems, in 1998. Women are more likely to be alcohol and or drug dependent than men, and they serve more time for drug or drug-related offenses (Snell; 1994, 1995).

Race is also an issue. As Robert Sharpe, a program officer at the Drug Policy Alliance in Washington, told the *International Herald Tribune*:[3]

---

3. Racial profiling on drugs, Letter to the Editor, August 9, 2002.

The problem of racial profiling in America is by no means limited to Texas. U.S. government statistics reveal that the drug war is waged in a racist manner throughout the nation.

Black and whites use drugs at roughly the same rates. Although only 15% of the nation's drug users, blacks account for 37% of those arrested for drug violations, over 42% of those in federal prisons for drug violations, and almost 60% of those in state prisons for drug felonies.

. . . Racially disproportionate incarceration rates are not the only cause for alarm. Children of inmates ate at risk of educational failure, joblessness, addiction and delinquency.

The disproportionately small number of women who actually are imprisoned (considering that they make up slightly more than half of the adult population in America), has led to a general neglect of the problems of dealing with the female offender. But the number of prison inmates is growing rapidly, and we need to consider that some of them are, indeed, women. U.S. Department of Justice Bureau of Justice Statistics reported (February 9, 2001) that if recent incarceration rates remain unchanged, an estimated 1 of every 20 persons (5.1%) will serve time in prison during their lifetime. These chances are higher for men (9%) than women (1.1%), but the proportion of female offenders is also increasing.

Some Facts about Women and Violent Crimes

At the 2000 Annual Meeting of the American Society of Criminology in San Francisco, a report by Elizabeth Dermody Leonard of Vanguard University focused on assaultive violence against women by male intimates; this is a topic of widespread social concern, and is the most common form of family violence.[4] Battering of women occurs in all socioeconomic strata. No racial, ethnic, religious, or age group is free from it.[5] Violence against women in the family is usually committed in private, so the actual rates of occurrence remain unknown. Rates which are known, in the United, States suggest that it is more pervasive than is commonly believed.

The U.S. Department of Justice reports that at least 4 million women are abused in their homes each year.[6] Intimate violence is ten times more likely to occur against a woman than against a man,[7] and numerous studies have

---

4. Levinson, 1989.

5. According to the Attorney General's Task Force on Family Violence, 1984; Bachman and Saltzman, 1995; Collins et al., 1999; Pagelow, 1984.

6. Hoffard and Harrell, 1993.

indicated a link between domestic violence and spousal homicide — battering can be the pre-cursor to murder. Of intimate homicides in 1996, nearly 3 out of 4 victims were women. A woman is most at risk when she attempts to leave or end the abusive relationship. Such women are at substantially higher risk of becoming murder victims than the abused woman who remains with her abuser.

- The National Clearing House for the Defense of Battered Women noted, in 1994, that up to 75% of all female homicides are committed by the victim's husband, boyfriend, or former partner.
- When female victims of abuse report the abuser and seek intervention by the justice system, they are often let down. And, among that small minority of women who go so far as to resort to violence in order to defend themselves, the justice system which failed to protect them later vigorously prosecutes the female victim for self-defending. Most of these women have no prior history of criminal or violent behavior.[8]
- Abused women who are accused of killing their abusive partners (72% to 80% of all homicides by women) are convicted or accept a plea bargain; many receive long, harsh sentences. Abused women who self defend are charged with murder or manslaughter and rarely plead self-defense.[9]

One of the women in our study (C8) commented,

"'Battered-wife syndrome' was not an option when I went through trial — my attorneys felt the abuse was a motive for the murder and didn't want it brought out. Yes, I had a Public Defender. Yes, they handled it different than I would have liked to have it presented."

Signs of trouble are many:

- Statistically, White women receive longer prison terms than do non-Whites for self-defense homicide convictions.
- Lawyers and judges involved in handling the women's cases often fail to invoke current self-defense laws which fit the homicide event.[10]

---

7. Buzawa and Buzawa, 1996; Edwards, 1985; Block and Christakos, 1995; Stout, 1991; Greenfield et al., 1998; Campbell, 1995.
8. Browne, 1987; O'Shea, 1993.
9. Osthoff, 1991; Ewing, 1990.
10. Magnigan, 1991.

- The National Clearinghouse for the Defense of Battered Women reported that, as of 1994, already some 800 to 2,000 women were in U.S. prisons for the death of their abusers.
- Studying women who used lethal measures in defense during an attack by their male abusers in comparison to other female prison inmate populations, we find that A) they were more likely married to their abuser, and were supported by him; B) they had fewer arrests in their family histories; C) they exhibit less substance abuse (except for alcohol); D) they exhibit notably higher rates of prescription drug abuse (38% vs. 21%).

Bloom's California study[11] corresponds to national survey data from which a representative profile of U.S. female inmates emerges. They tend to be 1) from very low-income homes; 2) disproportionately African-American and Hispanic; 3) undereducated 4) unskilled, with sporadic employment histories; 5) mostly young; 6) single, head of households, the majority having at least two children.

One inmate at WCCW told me, in 2001,

"I got here and I was crazy. My life had been hell out there and was it because of abuse? Of course. I was on the streets before I had my first period — home was more dangerous then the shit on the streets. I was used and abused, beaten, robbed, lied to, abandon. I think most women are abused — all the ones I know. When I meet a woman in here who says she hasn't been, I think she's in denial. I used to be too. Now I just accept it, it's the way life is. We're [women] basically almost all going to be victimized by men; if there are good men I'd like to know where they are, cause, I can't find one. Losers stick to me like glue and beat me down if I try to leave, or they just want to use me, so — "Janie

As recently as forty years ago, the problem of women felons was almost invisible. It may come as some surprise that as late as the 1960s, there was no woman's prison in Washington State. The fewer than a dozen women who were sent to prison were housed in a small wing of the Walla Walla men's prison. Today, WCCW houses more than 900 inmates.

Although there has been an exponential growth in the women's prison population, there has been no corresponding effort by Department of Corrections to consider the question of female offenders as women. The assumption has been that gender doesn't matter; they are just another minor element in a penal system. "Criminals are criminals." This is not simply a neglect

---

11. Bloom, 1996, p.69. For more information on these studies, see: *The Prison Journal*, Vol. 81 no. 1, March 2001 73-86, Sage Publications, Inc.

of the obvious; a great part of the psychological theory still in use either disregards, or even worse, mis-characterizes the psychology of women.

Watching the actual behavior of women, I was compelled to ask myself: Is there something about hormones and differences in the actual brain wiring of women that influences their emotional life? Do the politics of being female serve a woman or a man more? Do women (like the females of most animal species) have different relationships with their offspring, or are women so removed from their animal counterparts that they have no instinctual drives, and respond the same as men in offspring relationships and infant bonding? Do men stay in abusive relationships to protect their children? Do statistics show that women beat their partners as frequently as men do? Do women rape in the same proportions as men? Those were the questions that struck me about the women in the prison population: Crime seemed inconsistent with the rather ordinary women that they were.

> "See, when I cut my arm I bleed, and I cut my arm a lot because when I think of how they hate me, these strangers, the public, it hurts me so deep. When I'm treated like this, without rights, the whipping girl, I can't express my sorrow . . . so I cry . . . we cry a lot in here. Crying, everywhere I go, someone's mother, someone's daughter is in here crying, cutting on themselves, like me . . . Then we pray.
>
> "They tell me to stop it, like I'm doing it for their attention, but they are so far from grasping it — this inner pain that says, 'it's been like this all your life.' The beatings, the rapes, and the forced acts. I was trained so young to do what I was told. 'Take off your shirt, pull down your pants, put this in your mouth, shut up, stop crying,' and then all the things they did to me, but it was never 'them' that were the bad ones, it was me. That's what the system said to me in a hundred ways."— Tammy

It is interesting, if horrifying, that so much psychological theory has tended to reinforce a sex role of passivity as the norm for women. Carol Gilligan offers insightful analysis in her book, *In a Different Voice*, (p. 19). Presenting Chodorow's work and her argument of the masculine bias of psychoanalytic theory, she emphasizes that the issues of dependency and relationships are experienced differently by the two sexes. Males tend to have problems with intimacy in relationships, while females have difficulty with individuation. This characterizing difference becomes a developmental liability for females, as childhood and adolescent development are seen in the context of psychological literature that is largely written from a masculine perspective.

David McClelland, in his research on determinants of human behavior (1975), concluded that sex-roles serve as observable factors indicating sex differences. Further, he states that these differences have been evident since psychologists began conducting empirical research. The excuse for pushing that fact off the researchers' table is that it muddies the water, since human behavioral determinants are intended to speak for the whole of humanity. Findings are more succinctly presented by referring only to the dominate class; i.e., males. At the risk of complicating the studies with these differences, and attempts to avoid making judgments ("better" or "worse"), a single sex scale of measurement prevailed. This single sex scale has commonly been used by men, base on male interpretations of research data created generally or exclusively from studies of males. These studies are the basis for the standardized psychological "norm" test scores and the tests themselves are derived from them.

That women are identified as failing to "separate" and progress through the so-called phases of human psychological maturity are attributed in part to the work of Freud and Erik Erikson's elaboration of such work. Erikson (1950) posits eight stages of psychosocial development. For Freud, "Puberty, which brings about so great an accession of libido in boys, is marked in girls by a fresh wave of repression," essential for the emerging alterations of the young girl's "masculine sexuality" into the distinct feminine sexuality as an adult (1905, pp. 220-221). This he understood as acceptance of "the fact of her castration" (1931, p. 229). To the girl, puberty creates an awakening to "the wound of her narcissism" and forces her to develop, "like a scar, a sense of inferiority" (1925, p. 253). Erikson elaborates on Freud's psychoanalytic account, positing adolescence to be the period within which development hinges on identity, the girl comes to this crisis either in danger, psychologically, or with a different agenda.

Gilligan presents Bruno Bettelheim's (1976) illustrated archetypal conflict between father and son in "The Three Languages," in which the father believes his son to be hopelessly stupid. In this conflict, the father gives his son one more chance at education by sending him out to study for a year. The son returns, having learned one thing: "what the dogs bark." Two last attempts are made by the father, which the son fails, driving the father to such disgust that he orders his servants to take the boy to the forest and kill him. The servants, moved by compassion, decide to not kill the boy. They just abandon him there. Wandering the forest, he comes to a land infested with furious dogs who incessantly bark and keep the people from sleeping. Since they eat one of the inhabitants, from time to time, the dogs are feared and no one has a solution — except the boy who has learned "what the dogs bark." The hero begins to talk with the dogs and manages to quiet them. The boy has restored peace to the land, having learned just the right thing after all. He has emerged from this trial in triumph, having passed the test of his adolescent confrontation with his father, "a giant of the life-cycle conception."

Female adolescent archetypical conflict offers a pronounced contrast and is depicted by a very different story. A girl's first menstruation, within the fairy story theme, is followed by a sentence of intense passivity, where no action occurs. The sleeps of Snow White and Sleeping Beauty are periods of inner concentration, which Bettelheim considers to be the required counterpart to the "activity of adventure." These adolescent heroines awake from their time-out, not to triumph by vanquishing the scourge of the land or by conquering the world, but to marry the prince. This is their inwardly and interpersonally defined identity. For women, the world of fairytale depiction remains interwoven within the matrix of identity and intimacy. Bettelheim and Erikson view women, by their own accounts, as having identities rooted in intimacy.

Gilligan reinforces the gender bias argument by introducing Matina Horner's work supporting McClelland. In her book, *In a Different Voice* (1972), Horner finds that women typically experience anxiety when faced with competitive achievements, and shows that this particular response was problematic as it was a marker in a deviation from the so-called "norm."

Research on human motivation using the Thematic Apperception Test (TAT) has, since its earliest days, encountered perplexing difficulties with evidence of gender differences. These findings confuse and complicate data analysis. TAT offers opportunities for projective imagination by presenting a picture with ambiguous cues, from which the subject is to make an interpretation and complete a story, or a segment of a story. Psychologists then analyze the story to reveal the inner makings of the subject's perceptions. The concepts and interpretations offered by the subject reflect their experiential referencing within the world around them.

Even before Horner's work, researchers uncovered disparate responses between the sexes. Women were known to make sense of the world around them differently than men did, and when posed with competitive achievements, they interpreted situations from a perspective that aroused different responses.

McClelland saw a two-sided concept of achievement motivation, the "hope of success" motive to achieve success, and the motive to avoid failure ("fear of failure"). Unlike McClelland, Horner identified a third option: mitigation to avoid success ("fear of success"). This model accounts for the conflict arising between two motivations — femininity and success, the parallel struggle of the female adolescent to combine her feminine aspirations and early identifications with her "masculine" competence gained in school. Horner's study points to the predicament women face when success appears on the horizon. The conflict

25

stems from the potential negative consequences success can bring — threat of social rejection and loss of femininity — particularly when the situation is such that winning would mean making a male lose.

Georgia Sassen (1980) offers the rationale that women have a "heightened perception of the 'other side' of competitive success." This other side she refers to is the awareness that the concept of winning requires the cost of someone else losing. For women, this sensitivity and empathetic emotional knowledge can make a triumph bitter. Perhaps the notion of success defined as one-up-manship is particularly well phrased, for to whom do we attribute this perspective — a woman or a man?

It is a disastrous fallacy to think that there are no gender differences beyond the anatomical details. A woman's gender is as significant in social relationships as it is during medical treatment. To ignore gender when considering behavior can prove catastrophic when assigning culpability and intent to a "criminal" act. Yet, the court-assigned caseworker, someone who is not even a psychologist, prepares a pre-sentence report for every "criminal" case. This worker attaches a standard label as a personality flag of sorts, which will follow the woman throughout her life. This label has been coded to fit a particular crime based on "empirical" data polled from male subjects.

Mental Health Services at WCCW illustrated the problem in numerous ways. Women sent to prison were labeled by minimally-trained case workers who diligently categorized them as anti-social and as threats to the community, exhibiting longstanding problematic behavior (because they had histories of running away from home).

"The man just showed up at jail and said he had some questions for me . . . He had to fill out a pre-sentence report. I had no idea how it was used or what it meant. I am a 45-year-old professional, mother of two, and have never been in jail. I had no idea that the "system" could label me. The man asked about "financial problems", I had not worked for 2 months (due to my injuries from an accident), had mortgage, bills and children to support. Of course, that would bring financial stress so I answered yes (even though I have earned between $50,000 to $75,000 over the last 10 years). Well, I later found out that I was deemed "irresponsible" and likely to re-offend because of this. I had points deducted because I have no family, yet I have several people who support me emotionally (like surrogate family and friends) though my biological family is gone. There were many instances of gross interpretation if I had many friends, I could be perceived as having superficial acquaintances; if I had "few close friends" I could be perceived to be anti-social. Little did I know that this report could substantially support an excessive sentence, thus, handed down to me. Care needs to be taken to explaining the influence this has on the judge, as the report is wide open to interpretation by the clerical person interviewing the accused." — Debi Acey

These women suffered histories of neglect and abuse, and that was used against them rather than as evidence that at least some of their "problematic" conduct may have been highly appropriate. Similarly, their past relationships involving men with criminal records were considered as indicators of their recalcitrant sociopathy. Remarkably, these are the precise elements of the women's histories which point to a historical conditioning to accept continued abuse and exploitation by anti-social males. Are these female offenders mirror images of the testosterone-driven male offenders? Do these women harbor the same motivations and carry the psychological drives as men who commit crimes? The presumption was that they do.

If a male norm is the measuring tape by which we determine "deviancy," then female behavior is obviously deviant. Women who do not conform to the standards of psychological expectations are then victims of the obvious conclusion: since the women don't fit expectations born from male minds, something must be wrong with the women. Consider, for example, the case of Mary LeTourneau:

Case Study Questionnaire: Mary

Has sexual, physical or emotional abuse influenced your choice to commit a crime? (If you're innocent of crime, state so.) Did abuse change or affect your life? Did your abuse cause you to react to life instead of really thinking out your own behavior first?

I do believe that my sexual, physical and emotional experiences have influenced the direction I chose for my life. I chose to stay with a male that was (is) twenty-one years younger than me. In the state of Washington, it is a crime to be an adult and have a sexual relationship with a minor. In my case, because my partner was thirteen years old when our relationship became sexual, it is a "Class A Felony"; it is labeled as a "violent sex offense"; it is titled "Rape of a child." I do not see my life as anything unusual in reference to "abuse." So while I believe that my decision to allow my present relationship to develop was influenced by my sexual, physical, and emotional experiences — I do not consider my past experiences to be patterned with "abuse."

I am quite certain that "experts" in the area of psychology could find areas of my life as "abnormal" — and somehow fit my experiences into a scope of "abuse" — i.e. I was raised in an affluent, politically active environment. I was educated in private parochial schools; I was raised in a home that strictly adhered to pre-Vatican II Catholic practices; I married out of necessity (pregnancy) rather than compatibility and love. This marriage was very unhealthy and I remained in it for approximately eleven years. Even though my life memories are filled with much happiness and what I view as "normal" developmental experiences — because I fell in love with someone twenty-one years younger than me, I feel (and I have experienced) that psychologists and certain sectors of the public have scrutinized my life experiences out of context in an attempt to find some sort of "abuse" that gives "reason" to how I came to fall in love with someone so much younger than me (and a minor, at that).

I believe that my life before getting married was very healthy and I believe that I made very healthy decisions with that marriage for eleven years — my final decision being to leave the marriage. I do not believe that trying to work with the marriage for eleven years to make it as healthy as possible was "wrong." I believe that even though my efforts ended up in an "abusive" separation and that our overall compatibility was "unhealthy" — in the fact that I unselfishly worked to make it healthy was not a "sign" of any "maladjusted" childhood, or of some developed "personality disorder." Again, no "abuse" led me to my "crime." I am convicted of a crime [based on a law] that prohibits sexual intercourse with a minor outside of marriage. I thought about my decision to be in the relationship in terms of "moral" right and wrong, not in "legal" right and wrong. I did not know that my relationship had a "criminal" application to it. I knew that I was wrong in the eyes of my church, because I was not officially divorced before I began a new relationship. And even if I had been "officially divorced" — that, in itself, according to pre-Vatican II doctrine is a "wrong".

So in my family's eyes, I was disobeying the laws of the church — his age made no difference. So, as the state legal system defines it — I am guilty of a "crime" — Is that statute applied ethically to my situation? I believe it is not. Should psychologists and others be exploiting and examining my life experiences to try to "reason" what went "wrong" with me, the "wrong" being that I was convicted of a crime? No. I am happy with my decision — my choice of a life partner — but I am very frustrated with the refusal of the legal system to look at the case specifics of my situation — and I am frustrated with the media imagery and exploitation of my life — extreme distortions of my life. What happened regarding the relationship that brought me there, and the media's misuse of the legal terminology and classification terms attached to the statute I was convicted under — i.e. the title of the statute "Rape of a Child" and the term "sex offense. . ."

If court charging practices are at all influenced by society's assessment of deviant behavior, and if deviant behavior is qualified by the standardized "norm" established by the empirical data derived from studies based on male theory and male subjects, can we without reservation say our court charging practices are fair?

This brings us back to the crux of the mental health dilemma that women in prison run into: an inadequate assessment of their needs and an inadequate understanding of just who these female felons are.

> "In here, it's the same, so I cut, so I vomit, and it's all I can do to survive. It puts me in control of some of my abuse, just that little control, is that asking too much? I do it for me, not for them. I think about how the slaves were treated — you think about that a lot in here. Their struggles, the prejudice, and compassionless treatment of these people." — Mother of Two

The courts apply male standards of expectation to determine culpability, often with no understanding at all of what it is to be a woman in an abusive situation. As a backlash against the strides made by women for equal rights came the practice of prosecuting women as men. A poignant example of this sexist backlash would be a woman who killed, in what seems to her, in the actual situation, to be justifiable self-defense — yet she is charged with having committed the crime of murder. The rule of thumb goes like this: A person was killed; and it was murder, because there was forethought. The woman knew the man would come home and she had the wherewithal to obtain a gun. She had the option to leave but she didn't do that; and she never reported the alleged abuse, or if she did, she returned to the abuser.

The ordeal of the abused woman does not end when she is sent to prison; really, that is only the beginning. In place of the violent male, there is now an impersonal and uncomprehending system in which her pleas to be understood are merely categorized as evidence of her deviancy. The center of the system is the work by Mental Health Services to define her presumed psychological aberrance, and all of their testing and assessment are based on theories and data derived from males. The story of Vicki Cole is a good illustration.

When Vicki came to WCCW in 1994, she was a tiny, pale, good-looking woman. What I remember most vividly is her soft-spokenness and her desire to help the women around her. Over the years, as her health deteriorated, the severity of her condition showed — she could barely walk to the clinic. On a couple of occasions, I had to half carry her to the building.

For months, Vicki was unable to eat or hold her bodily functions. The excruciating pain from cancer eating through her bowels kept her bed-ridden and groaning in distress. Months went by, with staff denying the validity of her complaints. "Everybody's just trying to get more pain pills." We who had to watch this heartless drama feared for our own well-being. A few of us resolved to make the staff aware of the gravity of her condition, and finally Vicki was ambulanced out on an emergency basis to a real hospital. By then, it was questionable whether Vicki would be able to withstand even the first of the surgeries and chemo treatments she needed.

While we waited to see how long she had left to live, Vicki started talking to me about her past. She wanted someone to know the truth about why she had been sent to prison. She wanted to be certain that, even if she didn't survive, her children would know the truth of her life.

Given a prognosis of five years, Vicki was determined to find a way to help me in my work. In view of the fatigue she suffered, I trained her as an assistant TEC Betterment coordinator so that she could help me whenever she was able. She would come to visit the women in TEC and help present volunteer orientations and Quarterly Reports. The women in TEC immediately took to her. Having a wealth of experience with abuse issues, Vicki offered a comforting presence and empathetic manner.

When it was time for me to end my role at TEC, we had hoped Vicki could take over with another volunteer; unfortunately, by then her health was declining again. She has a wheelchair, today, due to other medical problems. She fights for every day; her children are her lifeline. Although there are no visits to maintain a full relationship with them all, she sees her son occasionally. It is not clear how much longer Vicki has, but for now she is with us.

This is her story, as she has detailed it in her pleas for assistance from the public.

March 20, 2000
Dear X:

I am in great need of help in my current situation of incarceration and I 'm reaching out to you in hopes that you will help me, or be interested enough in the circumstances leading up to my incarceration to lead me to somebody who will help.

My situation is this: I was arrested on February 18, 1994 and charged with 1st degree Felony Murder, by way of Accomplice Liability. I was tried and convicted by a jury, and was given a prison sentence of 20 years. I am also a First time offender and have never been to prison in my life.

I have been incarcerated at the Washington Correction Center for Women (W.C.C.W) since August 19, 1994 and spent 6 months in Pierce County Jail prior to my entry at W.C.C.W. To the best of my knowledge, I have exhausted all of my Appeal levels, except for the Federal level for which I have been told that my time frame for filing is going to expire sometime this month.

My Trial Attorney was Scott Candoo, (Pierce County Tacoma) and my Appellate Attorney was Patricia Pethic (Pierce County Tacoma). Ms. Pethic did an Appeal Brief for me in the Court of Appeals in Division 11 and in the Supreme Court where her obligation an, a Public Defender Attorney ended. I have been on my own every since.

I will try to be as brief and concise as possible in giving you the sorted details of the crime mentioned above and the circumstances leading up to my arrest and conviction.

I became involved with a man named Anthony Segura in about November of 1993 and I was 6 months pregnant at the time. I soon found out that Mr. Segura was heavily involved in drugs, crime, and the so-called "street life."

After staying with him for a short period of time, Mr. Segura became extremely abusive towards me, both physically and mentally, beating me into unconscious states throughout my pregnancy. I often pleaded with him, mentioning the harm being caused to my unborn child, but his reasoning was that "the child was not his, so he really didn't care." He also mentioned to one of his buddies that he was not going to allow me to keep my child once it was born.

At the first sign of any attempts to leave him, he immediately started having his "buddies" watch over me, keeping guard, so-to-speak, over me so I couldn't leave him. At one point I got an opportunity to call my sister, Sherri, but shortly after our conversation started Mr. Segura entered the room and grabbed the phone from me, stating to my sister that if she or any other of my family members ever tried to come and get me or find me that he would kill me and them as well. From this point on Mr. Segura relocated us almost daily to different motels, sometimes changing rooms 2 or 3 times per day.

At this point, Mr. Segura started injecting me in the arms (and sometimes legs, where the needle marks were not visible) with heroin. I had never in my life used heroin or needles before this, and throughout my entire ordeal with Mr. Segura I never once injected myself, even though I formed a "habit" from the drug and on many occasions was physically sick for lack of him giving me the drug.

On several occasions Mr. Segura would send me into different drug houses or motel rooms where drugs were being sold so that I could purchase drugs for him. He stated that, because I was a female, I could get a better deal than he could and he taught me how to bargain for better quantities. I was never alone during this bargaining and transactions; he was always very near by —outside of the house or room — and immediately intercepted me upon vacating the house or motel room.

On one occasion Mr. Segura took me to a motel called the Travel Inn on 25th and Pacific Street, in downtown. Tacoma. He gave me $100.00 and sent me into a room (#12 or 14) to purchase heroin and cocaine for him. I was told that I had better not come out with anything other than what he expected, because as far as he was concerned he had already taught me how to bargain and obtain "proper deals."

I went into the room and asked one of the Guatemalan men if I could get some heroin and cocaine. We did the deal, with me trying to bargain for a bigger quantity, but finally settling for what he gave me. No cocaine was purchased, only heroin. I took the heroin out to Mr. Segura and he then took me into the motel room next door where some buddies of his were staying. There

31

he and his buddy went into the bathroom and did the drugs, while myself and his buddy's girlfriend (Carolyn Westberg) waited in the entry area. Approximately 1 hour after the two men did the drugs, they then started talking about the drugs not being any good and they should go over to where I purchased the drugs to get Mr. Segura's money back.

From this point on, I was told to go get in the car and turn it on to get ready to leave. Mr. Segura told me that his buddy (Ronald Smith) and his girlfriend (Carolyn Westberg) were going to come over to our motel room with us and that they were going to gather up Mr. Smith's and Ms. Westberg's things and they would be right out. Upon my leaving for the parking lot to get into the car M. Segura told me that he and Mr. Smith were going next door to get their money back for the bad drugs that I had purchased. One of Mr. Segura's other buddies watched me get into the car and stayed in close distance until Mr. Segura and Mr. Smith arrived at the car from the motel room. Ms. Westberg came to the can shortly after I was already in it.

While sitting in the car waiting for Mr. Segura and Mr. Smith, I heard a single gun shot. I automatically assumed that the Guatemalan men in the motel mom were not going to give Mr. Segura's money back (this is common in any drug transaction, once you've made the transaction, the deal is done and there is usually no return policy). I assumed that Mr. Segura fired the gun either in the air or into the ground to let these drug dealers know that he was serious about getting his money back. But at no time did I ever think that the single gun shot that I heard was actually shot at somebody.

Approximately one minute after I heard the gun shot, Mr. Segura and Mr. Smith *walked* out of the motel room, both got into the back seat of the car, and I was told to drive back to our (mine & Segura's) motel mom. I never heard any discussion of the happenings that occurred in that room, nor did I know that anybody was shot and killed until the next day when I was arrested at a motel room that Mr. Segura put me in. Mr. Segura shot me up with dope and left me there. I never saw him again until the day of our trial.

I honestly didn't shoot, kill, or hurt anybody, nor did I rob or intend to rob, or even set a robbery up. I did what I was told to do by Mr. Segura for imminent fear of danger to my own life. The months I spent with Mr. Segura prior to this event gave me great cause to fear him, but I felt scared and helpless as to how to save myself from his overpowering control over me.

I knew nothing more of this event until our trial and subsequent conviction. I received an exceptional sentence downward to the mandatory minimum due to my 'minimal involvement in the crime at hand', quoted from my PSI Report. The prosecutor, Gerald Horn, had no objections to me receiving an exceptional sentence and stated that if my attorney were to propose the reasons justifying this exceptional sentence and alternative options thereof, he would not oppose them. However, the jury found me guilty as an accomplice and because my charge was 1st Degree Felony Murder the Judge, Mr. Donald H. Thompson, stated that he could not sentence me to anything lower than the mandatory minimum sentence for 1st Degree Murder, which is of course 20 years.

I might add that Mr. Smith never testified at the trial, even though it was proved that he pistol-whipped one gentleman in the room and threw another out the window. Mr. Smith received the same amount of time that I did, while Mr. Segura received a mere 6 years more.

I was absolutely shocked at my conviction, because my attorney kept telling me that I wouldn't be convicted because there wasn't any evidence to convict me. Nonetheless, I *was* convicted and then sentenced to 20 years in prison.

As if this whole ordeal wasn't enough, after being confined here at W.C.C.W. for only 13 months I was diagnosed with terminal colon cancer and underwent immediate emergency surgery to remove my entire right colon and appendix. I was told that they found lymph nodes that were invaded by the cancer and I was given a life expectancy of 3 to 5 years to live if I didn't do Chemotherapy. If I did do the Chemotherapy, my survival rate was increased by 30%.

I of course underwent the excruciating treatment and was able to stick with it for 6 1/2 months, as opposed to an entire year like the doctors wanted. I received treatments once per week for these 6 1/2 months, and then had the Portacath removed from my chest (which they inserted for easier access to direct injection of the chemotherapy into my bloodstream). The 3- to 5-year life expectancy I was given will be up on September 21st of this year. Which just happens to be my only son's birthday.

I have 3 children, including my daughter whom I was pregnant with when I was with Mr. Segura and despite his efforts for me not to keep her, I was able to by giving custody and my parental rights to my oldest sister, Donna Cole who has had my daughter (Stephanie) since she was 2 days old.

I had my daughter on January 16, 1994 at St. Joseph's hospital in Tacoma and the evening I had her, Mr. Segura came into my hospital room with one of his buddies and injected me with a large amount of heroin that made me see white spots and put me into an unconscious state. His buddy stood guard while Mr. Segura did this and all I remember after that was waking up the next morning asking to see my baby.

I was honest with the hospital personnel, telling them that I had been using heroin throughout my pregnancy, but not telling them that Mr. Segura was the one responsible for these injections because I was in fear, not only for myself but for my newborn baby as well.

Shortly after I awoke on the morning of January 17, (approximately 9:00 am.), Mr. Segura and his buddy came into my room and while Mr. Segura's buddy again kept guard outside my door, Mr. Segura had me get dressed and he and his buddy physically escorted me out of the hospital, one on either side of me, holding each of my arms. I made the mistake of asking where my baby was, and Mr. Segura told me that I was not getting my baby and that if I so much as turned my head to look at anybody I would be very sorry.

I was escorted to a car that was parked in front of the hospital, and once inside the car Mr. Segura gave me another injection of heroin because of my emotional state at leaving without my baby. All I remember him saying is: "Man, hold her down so I can get this into her arm."

I was now more helpless than before, after just having a child and given my emotional state — I was depressed, scared, and delusional. I feared for my life and felt I had absolutely no escape or hope of help from anyone. Mr. Segura's buddies were always close by and I basically gave up at this point on ever being with my family again. I was suffering from Post Partum Depression and was now heavily addicted to the heroin that Mr. Segura had been injecting me with over the past several months.

I will end this nightmare here with the closing hope of your help in my release from this hell. Won't you please try to help me? I'd appreciate a response from you either way so, please let me hear from you soon.

Respectfully & Sincerely,
Vicki L. Cole

Quantitative data recording crimes committed by female felons should be scrutinized for accuracy due to the faulty and misleading charging practices within the court system. Examples include charges of "murder" in cases of self-defense; charges of "accessory to felony" when abused women were conditioned to obey their male oppressors (many women would be beaten, even killed, if they refused to obey orders to keep their mouths shut and turned in the perpetrators); charges of every conceivable crime wherein the women refuse to testify against the male perpetrator for fear of reprisal.

When a couple is implicated, it is customary practice in Washington State to charge both the woman and man for the same crime and if the woman refuses to cooperate with the prosecution against the man, she is convicted of an offense equal to his. In an abstract way, that might seem fair; however, not only is it often the case that the woman is afraid to cooperate with the investigation because she fears reprisal by her male co-defendant, but her male co-defendant may accept a deal from the prosecutor to get a reduced sentence for testifying against her, when in fact it was he who took the lead in committing the crime.

Quantitative data gathered by surveys of female offenders is often misleading, too. Suppose a woman prefers to keep her personal history confidential — sexual abuse and battering, incest, or reliance on substance abuse to cope with her life — apparently, to record such events even in an anonymous survey provokes feelings of shame; or perhaps the survey respondents question the integrity of the data gatherer and suspect that any disclosures may somehow later be used against them.

Mental health opportunities within the women's prison remain elusive. Such services are extremely limited at WCCW, with only one psychiatrist, three psychologists and three social workers. The group therapies are primarily overseen by two social workers, as the psychologists conduct risk assessments and individual therapy for the more serious cases. Treatment programs are 12 to 16 weeks in duration.

To make matters worse, many of the professionals have been indoctrinated into the male model of reasoning and subscribe to it, the most insidious examples being a psychiatrist or a psychologist who would not be gender-sensitive and actively works to support and perpetuate the male discourse on rationality.

However, it was not subtleties such as these that first caught my attention, but simply the stunning state of neglect and abuse that characterized the health services at WCCW, including issues of mental health. While conditions have improved, prison resources are limited and professional care-givers are hard pressed to meet the needs of such a large population.

Cruel and Unusual Punishment Instead of Mental Health Care

The history of prisons is harrowing, from the practice of drilling holes in a prisoner's head to let the demons out, to lashings and whipping posts, to experimental medical practices, to today's practice of solitary confinement. However, other than the most hard-core sufferers from crimiphobia (that all-consuming hatred of criminals as polluters of society), most people would concede that medical service in a prison ought to be held to reasonable standards of care.

In 1993, a class action suit was filed on behalf of the women at WCCW to redress serious deficiencies in the prison's health care system. This case remains in litigation still. The following excerpts are from the transcript of this ongoing suit.

The Prison Clinic

- A patient left unattended on a gurney for the night fell off, during a seizure, and required emergency hospitalization. (p. 15, 1998)
- Patients wait for medication outdoors in inclement weather for up to 1 ½ hours. (page 16, 1998)
- A woman sliced a four-inch long, two inch deep cut into her arm with a razor blade while waiting on the med line, exposing the bone (p. 18).

- Medically necessary individual psychotherapy is not provided. The prison psychiatrist does not provide any individual psychotherapy, even to prisoners who are cited for infractions for self-harm and are referred to mental health services.

- Consequences include the worsening of symptoms of mental illness; self-harm conduct; difficulty following prison rules as a result of disorganized thinking; misperceived directions from staff; escalating agitated behavior leading to increased chaos and harm of others; and in the worst cases, suicide.

- Ms. M___ nearly died after a suicide attempt. Later, she testified to the harmful effect of the lack of regular individual psychotherapy on her. After her first self-harm incident, it would have made a "great difference" to her condition of depression, weight loss, and feelings of helplessness (p. 19). Fleming, Employee Report 899)

- A superintendent [from much larger men's institutions] stated that the rate of self-harm at WCCW is higher than the other prisons where he has worked.

- There have been a significant number of suicide attempts.

- In just three years, there were six different mental health supervisors. (Payne ER 432-433.) Key mental health-related staff who left their positions between 1996 and 1999 include doctors in the positions of mental health care manager, three prison psychologists and a nursing supervisor, a psychiatric nurse practitioner, the manager of TEC, plus one of the two mental health counselors in TEC.

- One of the prison psychologists said she resigned her position at WCCW, a position she had held for years, because she felt "hopeless." She could not focus on treatment anymore because she was distracted by constant staff turnover. During her tenure, she had five different supervisors and saw many of her colleagues leaving, feeling despairing and torn. She saw a "pattern" of good mental health people coming and going, and decided that nothing would ever change (ER 264-266.)

The mental health care manager left WCCW after 2½ years, because the direction of mental health programming changed frequently, the mission changed, and "I felt I was beginning to work in a very unsafe setting" (ER 239).

The exodus of essential mental health staff at WCCW accelerated after the evidentiary hearing. One of the prison psychologists left, soon followed by the correctional mental health program manager and the prison psychiatrist. The one psychiatrist had been hired during the hearing to replace the prison psychiatrist, who in turn had resigned in April 1999. During his short tenure, this psychiatrist commuted from Arizona to provide mental health care to women incarcerated in Washington (Robbins, ER 392-294).

As of 2000, WCCW has seen a shift in its administration. The former superintendent has been replaced, and the problems with the medical and mental health needs are constantly under scrutiny. This issue is often cast in terms of money, the claim being made that all would be remedied if the State would fund such services at a reasonable rate. And while it is true that Washington has no reason to be proud of its level of support for such services (the most glaring example being the scandal of the emptying of the institutions for the insane), still, conditions in WCCW were not just a matter of money. I discovered that, when I found out about TEC.

TEC is the acronym for a unit where women with the most severe emotional or psychological problems are housed. At WCCW, there are two units called TEC: Acute, and TEC Residential. The criteria for the Acute Unit include suicidal ideation reported to, or by, staff, or behavior such as cutting oneself. The residential unit is where TEC inmates go next, when they demonstrate job responsibility and no infractions. At the time of this writing, every woman in TEC is a mother, and their number one source of pain and complaint is their worries over their children. Most of the women were abused as children and were battered. About 50% were incest victims, and most don't have family support.

The following are court documents in which staff and inmates testified regarding the health concerns at WCCW. Bear in mind that these incidents all date to the previous Administration. They reflect gender differences that can show up when women are given the same treatment as men — many women have difficulty coping with this setting; they tend to internalize their anger, while males are more likely to externalize through aggressive action.

(ER 834-837.) The consequences of the chaotic personnel situation, with rampant turnover and overwork of personnel in TEC, are not limited to the deteriorated health services. Even while TEC was under the superintendent's close watch, a correctional mental health counselor had a mentally ill prisoner perform oral sex on him on multiple occasions, and threatened to kill her if she told anyone.

(ER 452-453.) Another corrections officer told a prisoner in TEC two days after she used a razor on her arm in a failed suicide attempt, "Next time, do it right"; and "Arteries in your neck bleed faster." (ER 178-179.)

Self-inflicted razor wounds are endemic at WCCW, and are increasing in frequency. One TEC nurse testified that, "It seems like in the last year or so . . . there seem to be a lot of suicide attempts related to sharps," particularly razors. (Reitz, ER884A.)

Self-harm incidents involving razors increased 111% from 1997-1998, and the number of serious incidents more than tripled. (ER 782.)

A.C___ slashed herself with a razor and nearly died. (ER 987.) Numerous other prisoners have inflicted serious wounds on themselves with razors. (ER 1002-1004.)

(p. 25) Grossly disproportional force is used against the severely mentally ill. Of 73 uses of force in 1998, 60 (or 82%) were against TEC patients, who are the most seriously mentally ill of the entire prison population. (ER 796.)

Use of force in TEC is so common that it interferes with staff's ability to provide treatment. (Wall, ER 417 38).

Prison staff consistently testified that intervention by a mental health provider can cause a prisoner to stop self-harming or otherwise de-escalate a situation . . . and reduce the need to use force. (Isham, ER 409.)

See also Video ER 982, videotape of inmate Ms. C___ drinking from toilet after being refused water by guards; mental health staff *not* consulted; agitated, Ms. C___ dives head first off toilet). *It has been a part of Ms. C___'s "treatment plan" to use pepper spray on her as needed.

(pg. 26) Custody staff in TEC pepper sprayed Ms. L. B.___, a developmentally disabled and mentally-ill prisoner, who was upset as a result of being denied a phone call to her dying mother. (Dearmon, ER 1034-1035.)

Pepper-spray is sprayed in the eyes and causes excruciating pain. (Isham, ER 405-406.) Its use in custodial settings has been associated with side effects including high blood pressure, nerve damage, chemical burns, and death.[12]

Prisoners at WCCW are written up with major violations for inflicting self harm. Punishment for self-harm infractions may result in loss of good time, segregation, extra work, cell confinement or loss of employment. Prisoners sometimes cry for help before hurting themselves, but their cries go unheeded.

On November 2, 1998, a prisoner indicated to custody staff that she planned to hurt herself. Instead of being seen by mental health staff, the prisoner was left alone, unobserved for hours, during which time she repeatedly sliced her arm with a razor. The self-inflicted injuries required 19 stitches. (ER 1046-1049.)

Staff recommendations for preventive measures against self-mutilation have been ignored (Johnson, ER 060).

Preventive measures were not taken with a prisoner who pulled the nails off all her toes and who has scars across her breast, on her wrists, and on her thighs from repeated self-inflicted injuries with a razor. (pg.28)

---

12. Cohen, *The Human Health Effects of Pepper Spray-A review of the Literature and Commentary*, 4J. Corr. Health Care, 73, 74-75, 82-83 1997).

One consequence of punishing prisoners for self-harm is to drive the symptoms underground so prisoners refuse to disclose suicidal thoughts. (Schaffer, ER 232.)

Prisoners who threaten self-harm at WCCW are placed in isolation, also called the Close Observation Area (COA), in cells that are dirty, cold, and devoid of any belongings except one blanket and a mattress. Mental health counseling is not provided in COA. Needless to say, prisoners perceive being placed in COA cells as punishment. (Wade, ER 382-383.) Such conditions can exacerbate a patient's mental health problems.

In October 1999, Ms. C. J___ felt suicidal due to issues related to past rape and abuse and was put in isolation after making 7 slices on her arm with a razor. (ER 187-188.) She was placed in COA for 4 days, denied underwear and denied showers.

Ms. N. R___, who is 19 years old, was placed in COA for 6 days and was not seen by mental health professionals at all after her initial assessment. Male officers watched her on camera when she was naked in the shower or went to the bathroom. She was not allowed calls or visits, even from her lawyer. The conditions in the COA were traumatic for Ms. R___, because she was raped at the age of 12. (ER 174-175: ER 1027-1028.)

In June of 1999, Ms. D___ was placed in the COA where she had an anxiety attack due to the small place. She was hearing voices and inflicted self-harm. She was not given toilet paper, even when she had diarrhea, and was not provided sanitary pads when she was menstruating. (ER 169-171.)

Ms. A. B___, depressed after the death of her child during childbirth, was placed in COA. (pg.29) J. O. ___ was overwhelmed by fear when placed in small room because of childhood abuse).

While in segregation, Ms. R___ cut herself and attempted to hang herself. By the time she was found by staff, she was blue and unconscious. (ER 1023.) This was her third suicide attempt. (Dearmon, ER 1030.pg. 30)

On January 36, 1999, Ms. C. T___ attempted to hang herself while in the segregation unit. The unit sergeant provided the unit staff no direction except to videotape the incident. Ms. D. C___ confined 23 hours a day in segregation cell, for more than 6 months, for setting herself on fire while in TEC.

Punishment of somebody who is in such bad shape as to harm herself is "gratuitously abusive" (Shaeffer, ER 232). Yet, asked whether she had received any counseling after three self-harm incidents, Ms. A. C___ testified, "No. Just sanctions." (p .36, ER 504.)

In August 1998, a nurse used the same needle on two successive patients. (Mergens, ER 1065-1066.)

The conditions reported in this document are staggering, leading one to question our social, moral and ethical practices regarding women and prison. The more I found out about this, the more forcefully compelled I felt to devise at least some small improvement in conditions in TEC. From that beginning came further work in other areas, which led to the study that is at the heart of this book. I believed then — and I believe even more so now — that it is possible to rehabilitate the female offender.

History has yet to demonstrate that the notion of "rehabilitation" is erroneous. After all, how can one be rehabilitated, if one is not provided the resources?

Perhaps the most disconcerting aspect of these reports is that the methods to control the inmate were designed for males. They are mostly legal and in keeping with policy. What needs to be reexamined is the reaction that is caused when such controls are used on women.

The conditions reported in this document are staggering, leading one to question our social, moral, and ethical practices regarding women and prison. The more I found out about this, the more forcefully compelled I felt to devise at least some small improvement in conditions in TEC. First came further work in other areas, which led to the study that is at the heart of this book. I believed then — and I believe even more so now — that it is possible to rehabilitate the female offender. This is less a secret between committed workers in this field, who know but have no power to alter the system.

History has yet to demonstrate that the notion of "rehabilitation" is erroneous. After all, how can one be rehabilitated, if one is not provided the resources?

Conservatives say that the failure, to date, to educate the female offenders into law abiding citizens "proves" they are anti-social and aberrant. No. It only proves that education as practiced in prison is not sufficient to achieve reform in the majority of female offenders — in part, because it doesn't take into account their different needs.

Prison education programs are financially handicapped, but by now there are many committed professionals and volunteers who know what needs to be done, if the resources are found to do it. The first step in setting a human being on the right path is to know what is wrong. For that, it is necessary to assess each individual inmate with care, based on a solid grounding in social psychology. It requires paying close attention to what the inmate herself says. That, I learned, was something rarely done within the criminal justice system.

3. DIAGNOSTIC DILEMMAS IN PSYCHOLOGICAL ASSESSMENTS

Because the diagnostic process depends considerably on clinical judgment, it is easy to label almost all serious offenders as having a mental disorder (i.e., Personality Disorder, Antisocial Type.)

The process of diagnostic evaluation requires a heavy emphasis on the clinician's judgment or the evaluator's opinion, so considerable care needs to be exercised in the rendering of this judgment. Unfortunately, it is easy to classify almost all serious offenders as having a mental disorder. This problem is discussed in the *Psychology of Criminal Conduct*.[13] Two interesting findings emerged. The first is that it is extremely rare for anyone to escape a diagnosis once he or she has been involved in the system. And second, 75% to 100% of the offenders in these studies were diagnosed as having a mental disorder.[14] It's not surprising that the disorder most cited by clinicians was the Antisocial Disorder.

The good news is that a prisoner with such a diagnosis is not at any higher risk of reoffending, (Feder, 1991).

---

13. (1994, Anderson Publishing, pg. 210)

14. The data used include DIS/Hodgins and Cote (1990), 494 federal inmates; Teplin and Swartz (1989), 728 jail inmates, 1,149 state inmates; Daniel et al., (1988), 100 females, 1,802 general population. ICD/Webster et. al., (1982) 248 court; Psychiatric Diagnosis/Guy, et. al., (1985) 96 jail; Cloniger (1970), 66 females. Level of Health Care Survey/Baskin et al., (1991) 3,332 male and female. DIS = The Diagnostic Interview Schedule. ICD = Word Health Organization International Classification of Diseases.

The hurdle to overcome, then, is ascertaining who in fact is "Antisocial," if it is such a freely used label? Are we over-labeling in an attempt to prove that we have a handle on the crime epidemic? If we categorize something, it feels less threatening and less unresolved. There is comfort in knowing that we can put these people in a neat file folder; they have been understood — they are antisocial. Unfortunately, that comfortable feeling goes hand in hand with an assumption on the part of the criminal justice system that these individuals will create another crime.

Recently, the Borderline Personality Disorder has also become an overused and misunderstood diagnosis — a label that can be used to sweep away clients that don't quite fit a clean diagnosis.

> The legal system in the State of Washington is backward. It doesn't understand or want to comprehend battered women and their mentalities — they automatically say that they are temporarily insane. The prison system is no different; they order you psych. ends., yet they have no information or 'real' help groups. You're left to your own devices. Community supervision is a joke. It's only to make sure you pay fines or pee in a cup. (A/P12)[15]

It is self-evident that America's penitentiary system was intended to prevent or discourage men from committing future crimes. But our entire approach to diagnosing, assessing, and responding to the problems exhibited by people who wind up being prison inmates (particularly females) is flawed at every step — as I have learned by studying the authoritative works in the field, as well as through personal observation. The next few chapters will examine some of the stumbling blocks that stand in the way of effective rehabilitation.

The inconsistencies that appear when examining an inmate's profile can be confusing: seemingly valid truths mixed with subjective and contradictory speculative theories. Having spoken with hundreds of women inmates, I was struck by the passive acceptance they exhibited when negative labels were given to them. It was as though they had given up hope of being anything but what their diagnosis offered. Many had been diagnosed by multiple case workers and psychologists, with each one assigning a different and new label to their file. The women would sadly repeat a long list of disorders they had been told applied to them. An example would run something like this: "I have borderline personality disorder and manic depressive disorder and narcissistic personality disorder and I am an antisocial that suffers from hysterical personality disorder." The first

---

15. Nearly all of the participants quoted in this book were willing to use their own names, while the research was being conducted; but I have assigned nicknames and codes now that the information is being disseminated more widely.

inmate who recited this inordinately long and excessive diagnosis left me baffled and jarred. It took a few more women reporting similar litanies before I recognized that these women weren't half as confused as the files that made up their profiles.

Only when I sought the general characteristics of their histories and discovered comparative factors that were consistent in their backgrounds did I arrive at the realization that, in almost each case, a history of abuse existed. In fact, it was uncommon to meet a woman inmate without a serious abuse history. Women and girls have often been taught, through their cultures, to please the male. Men control the economic resources, men have the power (financially and politically). Females are taught that their power is often related to their beauty and or their willingness to serve men.

The archetype of a beautiful woman, as defined by traditional American male standards, has been a combination of the child-like passivity we associate with the easy sexuality of Marilyn Monroe, paired or contrasted with the dignified bearing of a Jacqueline Kennedy. Magazines promote the frail waif like body of a pre-pubescent girl, hipless and with slouched shoulders suggesting an uneasiness with self-power. The era that bred these icons has left its cultural legacy on today's baby boomers. We bear the implicit lessons taught in a thousand subtle ways despite our knowledge that subjugation for women — as epitomized in the "beautiful" archetype — is fatal for female empowerment.

Lenore Terr,[16] an expert on memories and their power to determine behaviors, explains that people learn things without any conscious awareness of how they learned it; without conscious thought, our minds absorb information. This behavior, taught "implicitly," can be so strong that particular tasks are enacted by individuals without their conscious knowledge of just what they are doing, or how.

Most of us recognize "learning" as relating to something we are taught "explicitly." We focus our conscious attention on someone or something else that demonstrates how a particular activity is done. We are aware of striving to remember, to learn. When we are taught explicitly, we can explain what we are learning; we can identify this learning using words to the experience and we remember it.

So, what happens when a girl or woman experiences a life-threatening situation? What inner resources does she reach for, to escape the potential harm at hand? She will *think*, she will act, on what seems the best defense, perhaps by talking, crying, screaming, or striking out. If these first methods fail, she may have run out of the immediate reasoning accessible to her mind. What she

---

16. Author of *The Unchained Memories* (p. 44).

accesses cognitively is dependent on what she has learned, those things taught explicitly. Perhaps she becomes creative in her solution-making strategy, applying and combining this knowledge with that one. What happens when even these things fail? Is this when those implicit lessons become especially active? In such instances, victims will later reflect that "something just came up from within," guiding them to act in a foreign way. The response was "intuitive"; they can't articulate how it came up. It just happened.

In some fortunate cases, this solves the predicament and the girl or woman escapes the peril. And, if not? Psychology uses terms such as "dissociation" for the occurrence. The person has a sense of numbing out or checking out. When this state of absence occurs singularly, the victim can manage to come through the experience, alive at least.

> The crime I am currently incarcerated for, I am innocent of. However, I have been involved in criminal activities for the last 10 years (all of which have gone unpunished), and I do feel that the various abuses that I suffered as a child contributed greatly to my thinking patterns, which led to my life of crime and drug abuse. Therefore, yes, I do believe that abuse changed and affected my life and caused me to react to life rather than act, based on careful thought. (C9).

Going a step further, if the female is forced to remain in peril for extended periods of time and the peril ebbs away, but then returns, and the danger and drama are repeated, what is being implicitly taught as this cycle continues, is a learned helplessness.

Seligman, in experimental research with dogs, explored the conditioning response that occurs under unavoidable torment[17]. This conditioning in the laboratory, using inescapable electrical shocks, produced a response that had lasting effects. His subjects (the dogs) were cued by an outside stimulus, a light, to expect an electric shock through the floor. A few treatments of this, with the subject failing to find any way to avoid it, and the subjects gave up trying to jump from one area of the floor to the other to find an escape. The dogs simply resigned themselves to the shocks and didn't move; although they did empty their bowels — through a biological response to terror? Perhaps; or an attempt to insulate their bodies by using their feces to deflect the sting of shock; or both? Can you conjure any memory of a dog, under any other circumstances, choosing to lie on top of its own fresh feces? What might we do, as humans, to survive? Are women implicitly taught that social mores dictate lines and limits on their

---

17. Seligman, M.E.P., and Maier, S.F., 1967.

behavior — so much so that, what a male would readily assert as a defense against peril, women are less forward in asserting?

Do gender-based variations in hormones and brain have any bearing on this type of situation? Some would say, yes.

Seligman's subjects (dogs) maintained their reactions even when the light cue *alone* was given. They no longer needed an actual punishment to act out their defeat; no further electrical shock was administered, but passivity and resignation were absolute, without further abuse. The lesson had been learned.

I'm no different than the other women here. There was early abuse in my life, as a child. What makes me different today is that I've pursued, and obtained over fifteen years of various therapies. M personal work with many professionals has helped me to gain the clarity I have today. Maybe, also, I knew I was miserable and there as something that drove me to commit a crime. Later, in prison, I pursued self-knowledge. It's like when you're miserable enough, you have two choices here: either you get help or commit suicide. After awhile, the drugs and relationships couldn't get rid of the pain inside my heart and spirit. That's when you hit rock bottom. When I got there, I chose to get well, for me and my son.

Before the rock bottom, before prison, before the crime, I was frightened all the time, unless I could drug myself with medications. I felt so raw, mentally, that I didn't want to be around anyone. But then, I craved tenderness and gentleness. I couldn't begin to figure out how to get rid of my fear and still find a protector. I wanted the prince on the white horst to come and rescue me, put me in a castle with a moat. I wanted to be safe and guarded so I wouldn't be exploited and used again. I was willing to give up my sexuality and my freedom to pay for this protection.

I wanted emotional relief and release because I couldn't find it on my own. I believed I needed a man to help me. I believed I was not smart enough to make choices regarding my survival. All my past attempts to survive were so misguided tat I put myself into terrible positions. I didn't trust my power to think or behave. If I could just find the right man, he could tell me what to do, and he could fulfill my need for protection. He would defend me and guarantee my safety and he could take care of my fragile and tender heart. I wanted desperately to be loved but felt somehow guilt-ridden about being less than other women. I knew I wasn't as good.

I did notice that I seemed drawn to men that seemed strong or had a certain tough edge that demanded respect from other men (or that's what I thought). Once involved, I did all I could to be indispensable and serve their every need. It just made me feel better — safer, and loved. I didn't desire the thrill-seeking type, because I certainly didn't want any more fear in my life — I hate that feeling, and adrenaline. I drank and did drugs specifically to get rid of my nonstop jitters. I was always jumpy inside, and watchful.

I was never one to see my future in the far distance; I was too consumed with the day-to-day goings on. Whenever I was involved with a man, I never thought about abuse, per se. I mean, the violence, threats and property destruction was just part of the while that was my life. I would never tell anyone about the abuse; I always lied to the doctors in the emergency rooms. It was our business, and it was our sacred secret. Sometimes I deserved it and I thought, if I could just learn to let to, I could eventually feel something sexually. But I never did — it always just hurt. I figured the level of violence used was an indicator of how much they loved me. Their love was so powerful that they couldn't do anything but express it. Love overwhelmed them and they would lose control, because they loved me so much.

It was amazing how much I felt a part of them. I remember feeling guilty because I left them, as if they would be so hurt they couldn't go on. But of course, they did. It always felt as though I had cut off a part of my body because we had grown so closed and seemed to fit each other so well.

I can't say I grew to love them; no, it was like an instant attraction, like falling in love. It just stayed that way; I felt I couldn't live without them. We became part of each other. But then I saw that I couldn't live with them, either.

In each relationship I had, I always left with only the clothes on my back. I knew that if I stayed in the same state or city, or if I went back to any of our old friends, he'd find me and kill me. So I would have to start all over again — meet new people, find work and a place to live.

My dependency on relationships created a reality of men who used and abused me. I mistook anger for guidance, generosity with drugs or things that hurt me for love.

— Lynne

As the following case studies are reviewed, the expressed logic of some of these women will show that their view of the world appears to have an outer locus of control; it becomes clear that they see someone else as having all the power while they are mere pawns in another person's game.

Most people have never had the overwhelming terror and unfathomable experience of having absolutely no power in a life-threatening event; they can't imagine themselves susceptible to giving up, even refusing to fight for what is true. Nor do they believe they could ever succumb to pleading guilty for a crime of murder, or rape, when they are wholly innocent.

Recent cases in the news have reported death row inmates admitting to criminal acts they did not commit. Until investigations of DNA conclusively proved they were innocent, these prisoners had to undergo the experience of an "outer locus of control." Circumstances were such that they had no power to escape unlawful imprisonment, and their lying by way of confession indicts the justice system as the string puller, with them as the puppet. In certain instances and circumstances, there are greater realities that operate than the simple-minded one of right or wrong, good or evil.

There is an attitude, a point from which we reference the realities of the world around us. Frequently, we believe our perspective is the true, legitimate one and should apply to all, equally. Ethnocentricity characterizes such a view, a filter through which we see and take in the experiences of ourselves and assume insight into others' motivations. These views, attitudes, reference points on which we measure judgment calls are not easily identifiable in us; they can be our blind-spot, in that anything that exists beyond our views and filters must be non-existent.

If I'm in New York, but can't see you standing on your porch in Los Angeles, does it mean you don't exist? If it's raining in my city and I tell you, "It's raining," but you're in another city, and call me a liar, who is telling the truth? How do I make the judgment call, the assessment that rain exists?

You and I gather information and interpret it through our senses: eyes, nose, touch, and so forth, but it doesn't really stop there. We then define the impression using our past and current experience to find associations in our storehouse of memories.

All this may seem boringly trite, things you already know; and yet, there is so much of others we do not know. We don't hold their associations inside our storehouse of memories or experience.

Here's a quote from a WCCW inmate named Dutch:

> People don't "get" drug addiction. When I wasn't high, I was scared witless — I just wanted to stay in a dark closet and bang my head against the wall because there was so much ugly stuff inside. All the bad things my man or brother or society said about me, it was my fault. I made them beat me. I made men rape me — it was always my fault, and so I started beating on my own body, so I could stop myself from being bad and making people do bad things to me. Coming to prison was like — Wow, these fences and guards can keep those people away from me, now I can be safe. I had nightmares; still do. Sometimes, I wake up everyone in the cell block cause I'd wake up screaming like someone was killing me. If someone pushed their hair off their forehead, they'd lift their hand and as it would go up in front of me, I'd automatically pull my arms up to protect myself from the blow I expected, and at the same moment, I'd start to crouch. You ever see a dog that does submissive peeing? That's me. It was embarrassing — they'd talk about me like I was crazy.
>
> I think about suicide pretty regularly, but I have kids and I love them more than anything, I was told that it would injure them worse if I did that. I guess I figure it like this, I screwed up — I mean I don't hurt others or lie or cheat and I'm clean now, but I think because of my past I'm just damaged goods. If I'm

dead and buried my kids don't have to look at me or my past. They can move on, no dirt for their peers or the public to use against them.

Others here think I'm strong and kind — I don't have any enemies. I have a lot of support but, see, that only goes so far when society looks at us like we're freaks and bad seeds. It messes me up — to always be looked down on. It hurts bad. I know I'm branded for life.

By contrast, consider the self-image of Mary LeTourneau, who states positively that she was raised without abuse:

> I believe (and I am certain of this) that there is a silent majority that sees me and my case as a "miscarriage of justice." I feel bad that the government, and particularly the government of the state of Washington, has engaged in such a propaganda campaign against me that the silent majority is afraid to speak out because expressing the view of my case being a miscarriage of justice "seems" to be politically incorrect, and there may be repercussion in their work place of family circle that make life uncomfortable, and/or confrontational — which most people seek to avoid. I wish there was a safe way for this silent majority that I know is out there) to take a stand against what the government and the media have done to my case, and to me and my family. I am encouraged, though, that that silent majority is there and that they were able to see around the propaganda images and language that has been used against me by the state. Still, though, there are those that have been influenced by the media — some very distorted images of me are still being engrained weekly about my case, and more importantly the misleading education about the law — the statute that I was convicted under and the legislative intent of that law. Still, though, most of the public has read between the lines, or just plain ignored the sensational side of the case (and me) and for that I am encouraged for us as a people.

The contrast between the passive resignation of Dutch and the assertive optimism of Mary can easily be attributed to their personal histories.

In an institutional setting where the atmosphere is charged with a heightened vigilance for clues that will permit the pigeonholing of an individual, the possibilities for abuse, even in relatively benign circumstances, is great, as psychologist David Rosenhan demonstrated. To closer scrutinize the subject of diagnostic labeling, he conducted a test (Rosenhan, 1973).

1. First, Rosenhan selected eight normal, healthy adults: three psychologists (including Rosenhan himself), a psychiatrist, a graduate student, a pediatrician, a painter, and a housewife.

2. These participants were each given a script which they would repeat at twelve different hospitals. The script was this: they would individually go to the hospitals and state they had heard: "hazy voices" that seemed to be saying,

"hollow," "empty," and "thud." That's it, no more. Apart from this lie, each was to give honest personal histories.

3. One participant in this study was diagnosed as "manic-depressive" and the others as "schizophrenic"; in *all* cases the participants were immediately admitted into the hospitals.

Once admitted to the hospital, the participants stopped faking any symptoms and behaved normally.

4. However, in each hospital, the staff regarded everything they did or said as further signs of emotional disorder. In each case, the participants took frequent notes regarding the experiences they were undergoing. Observing this, several nurses logged the act in their records, without asking them what they were writing. One nurse logged, "Patient engages in writing behavior," as if writing were an abnormal act in itself.

5. The participants remained in the hospitals for periods ranging from 7 to 52 days. In not one case did a participant receive a discharge with her current state described as "recovered" or "well." The participants were each labeled as "in remission," meaning they were still sick, but just not suffering the symptoms of their fictional life-long disorders.

Rosenhan and the other seven participants, of course, never had a life-long disorder, but the study proved that anyone could certainly obtain one by just going to a hospital.

A psychiatric diagnostic label can yield devastating results — one of which is the "self-fulfilling prophecy," where the client tries to conform to the diagnosis, and where the propensity of a clinician is to interpret everything the client does as confirmation of the diagnosis (Maddux, 1996).

Even the DSM, the bible of diagnosis is not without its professional opponents. (The Diagnostic Statistical Manual is the tool used by psychiatrists and psychologists to determine the "proper" clinical label assigned to the subject's symptoms.) For one thing, the DSM staff who compile and create these labels continue adding everyday problems, classifying them as "disorders." The latest DSM IV version has a "disorder of written expression," and for people who have difficulties with math, they have a new label — the "mathematics disorder." Then there is the "caffeine-induced sleep disorder," a potentially life long addictive horror to coffee *aficionados*. That the DSM implies normal everyday problems are disorders which necessitate treatment is interesting indeed.[18]

The illusion of objectivity is a facade at the DSM. "There is an attempt to impose a veneer of science on an inherently subjective process."[19] Diagnoses are

---

18. Kutchins and Kirk, 1997; Maddux, 1993; Szaz, 1961/1967.

made by group consensus, not based on empirical evidence. In the 1970s when the American Psychiatric Association decided to remove homosexuality from the DSM as a mental disorder, the decision was not based on the research showing that homosexuals were no more disturbed than heterosexuals. The decision was made by a simple vote of its members.

---

19. Kutchins & Kirk, 1997; Maddus, 1993; Tiefer, 1995.

4. DATA COLLECTION AND EVALUATION — PITFALLS AND SUCCESS STRATEGIES

Historically, WCCW has been a neglected population for study. Female offenders have been considered the same as male offenders when it comes to setting program policies, institutional budgeting, housing construction and rules enforcement, with scant if any notice of the gender differences and histories.

For the purposes of this work, I have relied primarily on the qualitative strategy for data gathering, specifically, participant observation. Such field study methods and case studies are the only adequate method for obtaining accuracy in such a population. I also designed a survey to elicit information about the inmates' personal histories, attitudes, and needs.

While I also present quantitative data gathered by the Department of Corrections and other government offices, the inherent errors in attitudinal measurement of behavioral items must be recalled. Error of measurement (Deming, 1994; Phillips, 1971) may hold true as surveys and experimental studies include variability in response that goes unremarked and unaddressed. Then, there is the lack of comparability of studies, and differences which occur whether through bias, methodologies, design imperfections or other causes.

Any research is liable to error and bias, and I acknowledge this hazard. Have I been objective, myself? I am a woman, and I have experienced abuse

issues personally. I have been convicted of a serious crime. I have been rehabilitated. I have overcome an extremely dependent lifestyle based on co-dependent
and abusive relationships, substance abuse coping methods, and a criminal
expression of unresolved interpersonal issues. I now enjoy inter-dependent
relationships; I am free of abuse; and I utilize non-criminal behaviors to express
my inter-personal dilemmas.

This has been a slow, arduous journey and it is one for which many women
are seeking guidance. Charting the route and passing along useful information
has been a longstanding interest of mine. The study described in these pages was
part of my effort to draw up a road map that others may be able to follow. This
effort requires an openness to see what is, not what one would prefer. I have
made every effort to report and assess the data as it is, honoring its voice and
maintaining an awareness of my own bias, even as I work to set it aside. The
population this research is ultimately intended to serve are real people, not
statistical abstracts but women, with children. The interest of serving them is
my bias, the bias to provide a map and keys for those still struggling and
suffering in the wilderness, eating the ashes.

Quantitative Data

Presumably, prison inmates are assessed in relation to general findings. Yet
those general findings, the baselines against which behavior or attitudes would
be compared, can be deeply flawed.

Sussman and Haug (1967) demonstrated the gravity of unchecked errors in
the tabulation of survey data, including mechanical coding and data entry errors,
as well as sampling errors (the use of non-representative samples), and interpre-
tational findings that can reduce the validity of the results within a study.

And the fact of being under study can, in itself, distort the behavior of the
subjects. Orne found that his subjects were so willing to assist in an experiment
that he could not find *any* "experimental task" they would refuse to perform.
Humorously, one of Orne's obnoxiously senseless tasks was to perform serial
additions of rows of digits on paper and, when the subjects completed the
calculations, he would instruct them to tear up their answers and start again,
repeating the same task over and over. They eagerly repeated the task, without
objecting. There was no quantifiable limit, and Orne was foiled in his inquiry
(Orne, 1974, p. 142). The subjects were too eager to please to behave "normally";
one has to wonder, then, about the validity of responses in other studies.

Studies rely on two principal kinds of data: findings developed from
"artificial" research, derived from surveys; and "natural" research, the
compilation of data from statements expressed by persons in a "natural," i.e. not

contrived, situation. Can experiments be made so natural that they return valid measurements? Is "artificial" research prone to measure error, or the "error of measurement"? The debate goes on. For our purposes in this study, we will use the more natural methods of data gathering, bearing in mind that error is ever present in research and not exclusive to surveys and experiments. Perhaps, as some suggest, "The only perfect research is no research." However, in an effort to offer insight into the female population, even imperfect research is better than simple ignorance or prejudice.

Qualitative Data

Participant observation may be viewed as the beginning point of all other research, as Douglas (1972, 1976) suggests. Certainly, prior to designing a survey or any other experiment, we should first attain a general grasp of the subject being studied in order to ascertain what areas are most worthy of exploration. We also need to be keenly aware of any bias or preconceptions, moral or otherwise, that can influence what we see.

Participant observation has a long track record in the study of human behavior, and is a prominent method used by anthropologists in studies of preliterate tribes. Researcher studies are made within the groups' natural environment or setting, employing a variety of strategies while observing (and under certain circumstances, participating in) the groups' activities. As Robert Park put it in the 1920s, such field studies amount to "getting the seat of your pants dirty with real work" (McKinney, 1966, p. 71). Participant observation is used in ethnography, and is a basic component of ethno-methodology and field studies. Glasser and Strauss (1967) forward the "grounded theory approach," in which the researchers avoid artificially predetermining which hypotheses will be looked at; in this way the theory emerges during the data gathering, grounding it in the real world.

During the 1920s, the Chicago School of Sociology created a newly scientific approach to criminology and contributed to the early ethnographic work in this field. While such research has lost its once large funding, the Chicago School-style of research persists in being an example worthy of emulation.

To study criminals in their natural environment may be unwise, not to mention impossible, as leading textbooks on criminology by Sutherland and Cressey (1978) have suggested. But Polsky (author of *Hustlers, Beats and Others*, 1967), asserts a different view. And Polsky claims that moral objectivity is not necessary to gain a full comprehension of group activity.[1] Given Polsky's success in penetrating the inner sanctums of crime groups and individuals, his assertions make sense. Participant observation remains the major source of data gathering in police studies.[2]

Participant observation calls for a more inductive or sensitizing strategy than questionnaires or other standard methods. Weber (1949) used an approach he called *verstehen* ("understanding"), wherein the method or strategies purposefully engage the researcher in the role of the actors, in order to gain insight into the entire context and frame of reference of the subjects under study. He posited that qualitative research is absolutely necessary if one is to attain the subject's understanding of phenomena, based on the subject's perspective.

The various degrees or forms of participant observation are measured and defined by the level of involvement, of participation, relative to the degree of observation utilized (Gold, 1958), and are broken into four categories: complete participation, participant as observer, observer as participant, and complete observation. As a rule, in studying subjects whether through observation or participation, the researcher seeks to avoid influencing the attitudes or behaviors of the studied subjects. The most intrusive and, perhaps, most revealing of these methods would also be the most likely to disturb and alter the behaviors of the subjects under study.

Complete participation requires the researcher to engage in the group's activities and to actually manipulate the direction of group activity; it is also referred to as "disguised observation." Examples include a group of researchers who joined a doomsday cult in order to get a closer look (*When Prophecy Fails*, Festinger, Rieken, and Schachter, 1956), and a researcher who worked as a prison guard for nineteen months while gathering data (Marquart, 1986). This technique is rarely employed, as it may violate crucial elements of effective participant observation.

Participant as observer is a method in which the researcher generally identifies herself and does not endeavor to influence situations. This is what is most commonly meant by "participant observation."

Observer as participant may mean a short-term one visit interview.[3]

---

1. Polsky, 1967, p. 147.

2. Manning and Van Maanen, 1979; Manning, 1972; Sanders, 1977.

3. Holzman and Pines, 1979, clients of prostitutes; Cressey, 1953, *Other People's Money*/incarcerated embezzlers; Klein and Montague, 1977, imprisoned uncaught forgers, Letkemann, 1973, bank robbers and burglars.

Complete observation is participant observation which emphasizes unobtrusive measures to ensure as full as possible observation of the subjects without their being conscious of the observer. This would include methods such as viewing through one-way mirrors, and secretly monitoring sessions between prostitute and clients (Stein, 1974).

Seldom are any of these "ideal types" used singularly. Specific studies tend to blend these forms of observation, and then too, the determination of where one form ends and the other begins, is subjective and such distinctions between participant observation, field interviews, and unobtrusive measures can become arbitrary in certain instances.

One aspect that does stand out is the time and personal cost extracted in participant observation. As a general rule, such studies range from months to years, and some researchers report that they experience becoming a "different person" temporarily.[4] The researcher has to assume a dual identity during any exercise in participant observation, not to mention during "participation": the involved insider, the analytic outsider. Interrelationships and patterns of behavior must be objectively reported, without moral bias. Countless researchers have been asked, in effect, to "switch sides": to participate in the behaviors which the studies focused upon. Polsky was told he would be a good "wheelman" for a criminal's get-away car (1967); Skolnick was asked to play a "john" (a prostitute's client), serve at a bar, and offer advice on legal issues.[5]

Yablonsky, author of such field studies as *Synanon* (1965a) and *The Violent Gang* (1962), opposes the avoidance of taking a moral stance in criminal justice research. He openly criticizes Polsky's claim that moral objectivity is not necessary to gain a full comprehension of group activity (Polsky, 1967, p. 147). Arguments on both sides of this issue are well presented by Manning, in *Observing the Police* (1972, p. 158).

In support of Polsky's non-moralistic view, Becker wrote:

> In spite of the romantic yearnings of researchers and the earnest ideological assurance of some deviants, scientific requirements do not force us to join in deviant actions. But our scientific purposes often require us to hear about and on occasion to observe activities we may personally disapprove of. I think it equally indisputable that one cannot study deviants without foregoing a simple-minded moralism that requires us to denounce openly any such activity on every occasion. Indeed the researcher should cultivate a deliberately tolerant attitude, attempting to understand the point of view from which his subjects

---

4. Weinberg and Williams, 1972, p. 165.
5. Skolnick, 1966; National Advisory Committee, 1976, p. 131.

undertake the activities he finds distasteful. A moralism that forecloses empirical investigation by deciding questions of fact a priori is scientifically immoral Becker (1978a, p. 99).

The tendency of observers to over-identify with groups is reported in anthropological literature —such as an anthropologist marrying a cannibal chief, and others who take on the mannerisms of the study group — "going native," as it is commonly termed. Avoiding over-identification with the study group requires objectivity, which overrides personal subjective bias, *either way.* Malinowski, well known as an anthropologist, author of *Crime and Custom in Savage Society* (1926), *Argonauts of the Western Pacific* (1922) and other highly regarded studies of the Trobriand islanders, was regarded as a model of objectivity. Then, in the late 1960s, his personal posthumous memoirs (*A Diary in the Strict Sense of the Word,* 1967) caused a shock throughout the social scientist community: Malinowski expressed his true personal sentiments which turned out to include a profound sense of revulsion towards his study subjects. Prior to the publication of the memoir, it was assumed that he was, at the very least, neutral toward them.

Conversely John Irwin, who served a prison term before beginning his career as a criminologist, has been accused of romanticizing criminals. In his speech before the American Society of Criminology, Toby says (Toby, 1986, p. 2):

> Irwin talks about prisoners as though all of them are victims of an oppressive society. . . . And I can well understand that a person who has himself served time in prison is aware of decent people who, through adverse circumstances, committed crimes, were convicted and were sentenced to incarceration. I can even understand criminologists who, like Edwin Sutherland, get to know and become quite attached to professional criminals. However, loving the man and hating the fault is quite different from denying the existence of the fault because criminals are human beings.
>
> I think of criminology as a discipline. By "discipline" I mean more than subject matter. I mean that we ought to restrain impulses, including benign impulses, which prevent us from seeing the world realistically. Just as anthropologists cannot be trusted (intellectually) when they go native to the extent that they glorify rather than study their preliterate societies, so a criminologist who has gone native cannot be trusted to tell us what criminals are like.

Toby's speech underscores the need for a researcher's objectivity and yet at the same time reflects the precise attitude that it argues against: romanticizing a societal viewpoint (in this instance, the unequivocal rightness of our American society). In the event a researcher discovers irregularities and specious or equivocating rationales for a particular government practice or institutional practice, that should not be ascribed to disloyalty but to honest evaluation. Rather, researchers and practitioners reserve the right to present their own interpretations of the facts as they perceive them to be.

One challenge in designing, administering and interpreting the results of surveys is that attitude is not always directly reflected in behavior. Deutscher (1966) and Philips (1971) have both suggested "sensitizing" strategies that may offer greater accuracy. They cite LaPierre's "Restaurant Study" to illustrate the non-convergence of attitude and behavior: LaPierre accompanied a Chinese couple to 251 restaurants on the West Coast to observe the treatment they received. Only one restaurant refused them service. However, when these same restaurants were sent questionnaires, 90% indicated that they would deny a Chinese couple service. (That particular test would no doubt produce different results today, but the dichotomy is striking.) And F. E. Hage[6] discovered firsthand that the way a survey is conducted can affect the results. In the early stages of a rural survey, an inordinate level of fear of becoming crime victims was expressed by the survey population. It turned out that one of the interviewers, an elderly woman who had recently been a victim of crime herself, unconsciously led her respondents to perceive or to state that crime was a primary problem for their community. The distortion was corrected and did not damage the study, but it had the potential to do so. Any number of biases can compromise studies at every stage, and objective evaluators are needed to analyze program outcomes.

Inaccurate results can also emerge through design imperfections in either the analysis or the instrument. Unaccounted-for nonrespondents may differ from those who cooperate in a survey. If such a factor is not understood, the results of the survey may prove inaccurate and compromised.

One moderately useful way of dealing with the potential for error is to acknowledge one's biases in doing and recording the research. A bias is more than simply a consciously held perspective. It comes as much from the history of the individual as from her consciousness. Finally, it is for the reader to assess the author and her work, not to achieve some "objective" truth, for the reader carries a history and biases too, but to integrate the author's work into the reader's consciousness.

Like Polsky, I believe we have relied too much on studies of imprisoned criminals in an unnatural environment and on unquestioned use of official statistics. This has hindered the sociological process of effecting change in a huge and ever-growing segment of our country's population.

---

6. Author of *Research Methods in Criminal Justice and Criminology*, 1972.

My study emphasizes qualitative data, and follows basic rules of moral objectivity. As for observer objectivity, versus "going native," although I share many common elements with the study group "Female offender incarcerated," I have been rehabilitated. The unusual advantage of having first-hand experience in abuse issues and crime enhances my validity as a researcher. I have come through the circumstances and common dilemmas these women have undergone, and with the help of therapeutic assistance and emotional support systems, and years of research and self-study, I have become conscious of the natural bias of the victim-offender mentality that is so prevalent among this study group; and I built the mental strength to be able to turn that off. It is precisely due to my own rehabilitation and those advantages that I have enjoyed that I now am compelled to address this area of study.

As for the importance of perceptions, and even perceptions of our perceptions, I include two responses to the survey question, "What do you think the public thinks about you, and why?"

> "I think, based on the recent court decisions and lobbying being done, that the majority of the public sees me as a convicted felon, as being not worth saving, unredeemable. It seems like people do not realize that I am human, intelligent, and no different than they are. I just made some bad choices and want another chance. They don't think of me as a mother, a daughter, a sister, and a worthwhile human being with something to contribute to the world. I am not a number." (C9)

Data Used in this Study

This study is fundamentally based on the extensive and detailed field notes that I have recorded and analyzed over a period spanning more than fifteen years, and a collection of 40-plus photographs and paintings which illustrate particular issues.

Mnemonics, anagrams, and tape recordings have all been an essential part of my work, particularly when situations have been observed in which litigation was imminent.[7]

Smykla, an American Fulbright scholar doing research in Uruguay, described his initial goal as "inoffensive social interaction." By mastering that approach, one can earn the subjects' trust and discover various insider nuances that need to be learned, while avoiding the pitfall of forcing the researcher's own

---

7. See, "WCCW inmates versus Superintendent Payne," court document brief in admissions file TESC.

agenda and preconceptions onto the subjects or allowing them to influence the study.[8] Of course, I had a certain advantage in that my history at WCCW has afforded me entry into all segments of the population. I have the distinction of being not only a peer, but also a "convict" lifer who has authentically rehabilitated herself into an educator and activist for the benefit of this community.

Gaining access to the closed population of TEC was hard earned and was possible only due to my reputation for integrity (in my dealings with staff and administrators of the prison, as well). My relationships with the gatekeepers (as they are referred to), aided by my *announcement of intentions* to develop specialized programs to meet their mental and emotional health needs, i.e., the women of TEC, helped persuade them to open up to me.

Sampling was accomplished by the "snowball sampling technique." To inspire trust among the subjects, I revealed personal elements of my own life and discussed the history of my work within the prison — now over two decades. As I became privy to incidents that, by their nature, could cause trouble for the participants if the authorities were informed, I was in effect tested for trustworthiness. Since I chose to not betray the confidences of the participants, my status as a "safe" confidante was established. The ethics involved were at times conflicting: prison officials permitted me to enter and interact with the most sensitive of inmates, who were at risk for self-harming behaviors, and I had a duty to report any such incidents or any vocalized plans to do so. However, in order to impact and assist these participants in the activities which could help foster behavioral changes and more positive attitudinal beliefs about themselves, which "officials" are unable to offer by the nature of their position, I had to earn the participants' trust.

To stay true to both groups, I developed a unique arrangement with the unit's supervisor and the sergeant. Directly after my unit visits with the inmates, I was given an immediate opportunity to confer with either one, on terms that were negotiated in advance. When I did request such a debriefing, I was not required to identify the source of my information and that in the case of contraband items, which were, indeed dangerous. I could act as an intermediary for staff. By my one-on-one talks with high-risk participants, I was often able to encourage them to turn in the contraband to the sergeant — under the agreement the participant would not be punished but commended for this leap of faith in reaching out to others.

Reciprocity and protection of identity requires an agreement on mutual obligations. Research subjects assist the investigator and the investigator offers an incentive. In this instance, the subjects openly disclosed their thoughts,

---

8. Smykla, 1989, p. 29.

histories and fears while expecting respect, empathy, and assistance — where possible — in their communications with officials. Additional benefits were increased activities and exposure to new stimuli as well as opportunities for interpersonal growth.

Protection of informant identities was agreed upon, to reduce risk of retaliation. Risk to the investigator could result, if the integrity of the agreement with the subjects was violated.

Accuracy and validation of informant testimony must be assessed. My data validity was assigned a value, highest to lowest, based on a model adapted from Ianni and Ianni.[9]

Assumed Validity	Means of gathering information
Highest	Data obtained by direct observation during our active participation
Very high	Data obtained by direct observation, without direct participation
Medium	Interviews which had corroborating sources with documentation, institutional paperwork, court documents, staff verification.
Less reliable	Data corroborated by more than one informant
Least reliable	The lowest validity rating was given to data derived from only one source other than myself.

In addition, a modified version of Steffensmeier's validity checks[10] were implemented to cross-validate the reliability factor:

1. The interview structure incorporated a cross-check by rephrasing questions and repeating questions in subsequent interviews.
2. Documents were compared, e.g., newspapers, infraction reports, and letters.
3. Observation outside of interviews was considered: feedback from peers and staff.
4. Interviews were conducted in dayrooms, private areas and via group discussions in cafeteria or recreation areas.
5. The data were checked for consistency with biographies and autobiographies of female felons.

Those whose scoring and background interviews with others and whose documents proved consistently reliable were selected as the core focus of this study.

---

9. 1972, pp. 188-189.
10. *The Fence: In the Shadow of Two Worlds* 1986, pp. 4-6.

5. POCAAN and Peer Education

Effective Programs in Correctional Education —
Applying the Principles in Practice

> "The single most satisfying thing to me is helping people of a less fortunate nature, such as the mentally challenged and people who have locked themselves into a shell. Nine times out of ten, it is people like this who are extreme victims, whose innocence has been taken in one or more forms." (C4)

The first time I officially facilitated a program was in the Department of Corrections, in 1988. Implemented under a federal grant, the People of Color Against Aids Network (POCAAN), based in Seattle, was initially a community-based program to address the AIDS epidemic, and this was expanded into the prison system. The program targeted women at high risk for transmission and, using research and demographic studies by the Center for Disease Control (CDC), POCAAN easily identified WCCW as a target group for intervention. These were women whose behaviors — unprotected sex, employment in the sex industry, substance abuse histories, IV drug use, poverty, and so forth — made them particularly liable to contract HIV (and other infectious diseases).

POCAAN's Mission Statement

To develop implement and promote comprehensive multicultural HIV/ AIDS prevention models that are effective and responsive to the evolving needs of communities of Color.

POCAAN's Purpose

To respond to the HIV/AIDS epidemic that has a devastating impact on communities of Color.

Once POCAAN began their pilot program in 1988, peer education began. This was a wildly revolutionary step for the institution which, as an unspoken rule, routinely undermined any efforts by the women to take on any authority capacity that might empower one of the prisoners within the small prison community. By the unusual demands of peer educating (social trust, role modeling, maintaining of confidentiality, communication and specialized training by outside sources) a radically different and innovative program was offered.

Peer Education was implemented by enlisting members of this target population to act as educators and to provide support for behavioral change among their peers.

Peer educating, in this model, allows the resources already in the prison to be used: the inmates. While various duties and skills are honed, an internship period goes on, until they have graduated from the study and have gained hands-on experience. The person serving as peer educator becomes a social role model, which inspires others to make an effort in the same direction. "Peer" means someone from the target group.

That the program is officially recognized aids in building the peer educator's self-confidence and esteem. In this segregated population, the segregation not limited to their criminal conviction status. The inmate's segregation began before the crime.Some causes of this segregating have to do with the lack of opportunities to gain the social skills to fit in with the "mainstream." Unfortunately, those popular media portrayals of women who are able to survive abuse and addiction and then rise to the level of a functional law-abiding citizen, are the rare exceptions, not the rule. If this truth were made more apparent, that it is the "exception" to the rule, the rare case indeed, that succeeds without intervention — the bias against these women would decrease.

"This place has done nothing to aid in my rehabilitation. At most, it has helped in destroying my self-esteem. It has made me resentful and angry. They have done nothing to address my mental health and other abuse issues. Their answer to my problems is to medicate me. This place is supposed to rehabilitate me, yet I am deprived of any real education, beyond a G.E.D. or office training. I mean, really, do you think I'm gonna come out a better person when I'm constantly being put down and treated like I'm less than a human being? I'm not receiving adequate education and instead of giving me some therapy or one-on-one counseling, I'm just being medicated. I need mental help and an education and some positive reinforcement to leave here successful. We need more guidance, through self-help courses." (AA21)

The peer leadership position is intense, and often demanding; and it necessitates organizational skills and proper methodology to handle data collection. After every contact, the peer educators are required to complete various forms: attendance counts, ethnicity, ages, time, date, location, facilitators involved, hours engaged, topics presented, tools used, follow-ups and calendar appointments, locating and distributing text-resource materials and clinical data, and then making sure enough hand-out information was on hand for the next session.

After each presentation, participants were asked to take a post-test (for our evaluative purposes only), and then provide feedback on their general impressions or comments about the presentation and facilitators.

Implementing POCAAN

When the POCAAN program was brought to WCCW, the implementation began with applications, interviews, training, testing of potential candidates to serve as Peer Educators. The screening process eventually culled five inmates from the large number of applicants. Intensive training began, and was conducted over a three-month time frame. Particulars of this training were related to AIDS/HIV as well as to other Sexually Transmitted Diseases (STDs).

The nature of peer education is demanding (it requires communication skills, accuracy in data gathering and reporting, a strong adherence to rules of ethics, and the poise and personality to conduct a workshop with participants who are not used to that sort of activity). The candidates were highly motivated, however, and they did effectively reach the desired level of competence. Training was ongoing throughout the year, in collaboration with NorthWest Family Center, King County's Health Department, King County Women's HIV/AIDS Task Force, The University of Washington, and the Center for Disease Control.

Peer Educator duties and responsibilities included giving group lectures and slide presentations of case studies, along with demonstrations of how to use condoms and dental dams, and discussions of non-oil lubricants, the use of Saran

Wrap in sex, latex gloves etc.), for all incoming inmates, weekly. Additionally, these volunteers created seminars and did research as needed on subject matter that had been requested for open-population meetings with the WCCW Infectious Disease Nurse. Quarterly training sessions and testing were also required, and reports were to be completed and statistics kept on each contact, based on survey questionnaires that were filled out by participants at each presentation. Peer Educators could also be asked to serve as a peer support counselor for women with HIV/AIDS or a terminal illness. As a paramount consideration, Peers were to abide by the tenet, "Do No Harm," and take particular care to maintain confidentiality.

Serving as peer educator for over eight years, between the years of 1988-1996, I calculate that I gave some 400 presentations, attended by a minimum of 8 and up to a maximum of 70 inmates. It was WCCW policy that all incoming prisoners receive some briefing on these critical subjects. As a result, I had contact with some 3200 female inmates through this program, alone.

- The study that lies at the center of this book was based on a population that included those 3200 and others who had contact with these programs, in other words, those who:
- Attended mandatory POCAAN Orientations (from 1988 through 1995, this was a part of the institution's Orientation Agenda for all inmates coming in).
- Signed up for open-population POCAAN seminars.
- Attended AVP workshops or support groups 1996-2000.
- Participated in any of the TEC Betterment Programs, whether as facilitators or participants. TEC Betterment facilitators were interviewed weekly, and their remarks were transcribed for review (50 women); TEC participants were seen daily; their issues were brought up on an as-needed basis, and their remarks were recorded as anagrams or field notes (50 women).
- Responded to surveys, answered questionnaires with direct questions, writing their remarks (131 women).
- Participated in Case Studies and answered questionnaires, responding to direct questions in written remarks and repeat interviews (4 women).

Total contacts, for the purpose of work, were 4253. Inmate totals will vary.

Of these women, 3000+ responded in writing to questionnaires from POCAAN and AVP, in which they were asked to comment on their personal needs or areas in which they desired further information. (Issues such as standard GED or college educational studies, legal advice, custody issues and other topics not relevant were excluded.)

The Special Needs Unit

During the late 1980s, my first program for the mental health unit (at that time called the Special Needs Unit, or SNU) was approved: The Out-Reach Program. The Out-Reach program consisted of a small group of model inmates who were pre-screened by staff. The criteria for participation were difficult to meet, so only five inmates were admitted.

Our activities were monitored. Strict guidelines were to be met: do not discuss complaints about staff or institutional issues, no legal issues, no religious preaching. Activities were limited to coloring, and letter writing.

The limitations left a lot to be desired. The exclusion of certain volunteers who had more experience with depression or acting-out behaviors (an institutional term which means an inmate's behavior is out of control, or rebellious) meant that women who could uniquely represent a positive model of peer success were unable to serve as volunteers, essentially decreasing the effectiveness of the Out-Reach Program. We found the great effectiveness of using women who have also experienced depression and similar histories, yet came through it; in other words, those most sympathetic and personally knowledgeable. They seem to inspire and motivate those who are still struggling

The Out-Reach Program remained active for over a decade, though it fluctuated in its activity level. While it failed to make the impact hoped for, it was a promising start.

In 1996, I was determined to start a new program at the renamed "TEC" unit. Having seen how the limitations imposed by administration had inadvertently undermined the work's effectiveness, I determined to try something different. After numerous requests, I was finally granted access into this high-security closed-population unit in late 1998. I worked alone, initially, until I could gain credibility with the staff and prove my intentions and abilities.

In the next phase of the project, as coordinator, my goal was to utilize ex-residents of TEC as volunteers so that they could gain self-esteem by being the ones helping others in need. They acted as role-models and inspiration for current TEC residents.

"In TEC I sat back and talked with all the women and they told me their stories. I played games with them, watched TV; we really did a lot of one-on-ones, and it was very emotional sometimes. Sometimes I dumped on them and they supported me and helped me, too. I felt a lot of them were very intelligent. We went though cycles of that.

There were a couple of women with whom I got particularly attached. One lady never talked to anybody. She was here for killing a family member. She told me how her family really messed her head up. At first she wouldn't talk to anybody, not even me. I started playing "name that officer." I'd imitate the officers; and they were laughing, and then out of the blue she named the officer I was imitating, and our friendship started from there.

I went to TEC as a volunteer, because I was bored and needed something to do. I was the kind of person who likes people. I worked at Children's Hospital, with the AIDS children, and at Harbor View Medical Center.

In TEC, those women helped me understand that we're all children; there's a child in all of us and we just have to let that child out and be ourselves. The people around me in the dorms (TEC), we're all in bondage, yet when we were together it got so peaceful. I love working in TEC with those women. I love those women, and they love me."

—Tonya

This type of example provided hope in an environment that negated the inmates "okayness." Knowing one's limitations is essential to mental health; however, imposing limitations that can one day be overcome is another matter.

The team of volunteers was ethnically diverse, as were the TEC residents. The hardest aspect was to hear the pain and stories of these women's lives, the injustices and abuses that left these human beings with shattered self-images, emotional misery, and despair. There were times when the women had self-injured only hours before I saw them, and they would show me stitches on their bodies, 40-stitch, 80-stitch wounds.

While some women were impaired too severely to regain autonomy in the community, I think most, with proper treatment and new skills, could manage productive law-abiding lives. My focus on recovery has been intensive and my personal goal has been to enrich other women's lives in a supportive and beneficial way. In recognizing the talents of women here, I sought to facilitate programs which could put these skills to use. Such volunteer involvement has double benefits, of course: first, to the volunteers whose attributes are validated and beneficial to others, and second, to the recipients of their volunteer work. WCCW has many inmates desirous to be of service to others, and they are a resource still waiting to be tapped.

The TEC Betterment Program operated from Fall 1998 through 2000. During its development, first referred to as TEC Reading Program, with only myself admitted in, the program expanded into poetry workshops, recitals, chapbooks and essay writing. The TEC Mural Program developed, creating large murals for the general population and a mural donation for a DOC fundraiser;

the TEC Music Program brought song and dance which also was used in Unit productions. The TEC Betterment Program was the umbrella for these and other activities which included general-population posters made by the TEC inmates, providing upbeat thoughts and pictures; letter writing, one-on-one talks, certificate awards for staff and inmates and other incidentals. We served TEC seven days a week, twice daily, 365 days a year.

Throughout its work, approximately fifty inmate volunteers facilitated the Betterment Program's work. I served as coordinator. My work was to create and develop the programs, recruit and screen volunteers, train and oversee the operations, and remain active as a hands-on volunteer.

The TEC Betterment Program will be discussed in greater detail in later chapters.

Peer education is the key to reaching this population, and has proven effective in transmitting essential information.

During my first years of peer service with POCAAN, I recognized the women's need for solid, basic, accessible education in life skills and in formal academic studies in writing, reading, social studies, history and math. The humanities were nonexistent in their lives. When I speak of accessible education, I mean that they need to be taught by teachers who are able to meet their cultural norms in metaphor, analogy and language; many of these students are not proficient beyond an 8th grade level. The women made this need for schooling apparent through their comments on the questionnaires, and by identifying which of the peer educators they learned the most from. It is no wonder: those peer-educators who had the flexibility to learn not just standard English but the language of the people they sought to teach were the most effective. Test scores (post-testing) revealed what might be, on a larger scale, if teachers were taught how to teach from their students' own intellectual reference points, and the cultural associations from which analogies can be usefully drawn.

Research studies by POCAAN were presented to federal offices in Washington D.C. in 1996; their findings reported that peer educators not only conveyed the subject matter intended, but were found to influence behavioral norms. The community respects the messenger who brings them real information that will enhance their well being, or knowledge which is free and valuable, who performs activities for the community's benefit honestly and with respect for the audience backgrounds.

Through the easy accessibility of a peer educator, newly acquired ideas, attitudes and behaviors are reinforced by familiarity, frequency of contact, role modeling and trust. The role modeling and training we offered was designed to provide opportunities for participants to experiment with new concepts and attitudes about their selves and others; it is geared at long term change.

Segments of this population who would not engage with the "System" often engage with certain of the peer educators. Not all peer educators have the same personality or style of communication. There are some identifiable traits which the more popular peer educators (judging from requested one-on-one contacts and participants' comments) possess. Descriptions of a "popular" educator include: "She breaks it down so I could understand it." "She really cares about us, she was open and up-front." "She made it great to listen to — and she listened to all of us, too." "She walks her talk; made me feel good — no bullshit." "She had a hard background, but showed me that even I could make it." "She inspired me to be like her." "She made me feel good about me."

The peer educator necessarily enters the population's untouchable segment of IV drug users and others involved in high risk behaviors. All these women are not only the highest risk of contracting a sexually transmitted disease or suffering violence, upon release they are also at the highest at risk of committing new crimes and returning to prison. This target group of the population needs to be addressed for pro-social empathy work and reconnection to the outside community through bonding activities. They need special care to show them that they can share responsibilities and enjoy the privileges that go with it.

6. THE ALTERNATIVES TO VIOLENCE PROGRAM (AVP) AND PEACE TALKS

Alternatives To Violence (AVP) is an internationally active non-profit organization, with its headquarters in Texas. The AVP Program was created by the Quakers, and evolved with the collaboration of inmates. It was an experimental program created in response to the riots of the 1960s, but was found to be highly effective in a variety of settings, and as it became more widespread, its structure was refined. It has recently been replaced by Peace Talks, in which an updated gender-defined model is used; the weekend format has similarities.

As a Lead Facilitator for AVP, I designed and conducted 3-day workshops in communities both public and private). The AVP work was originally intended for male inmates, and the standard manuals were used for both genders. I collaborated with other facilitators to create new exercises, and have created some of my own. Some of the exercises from our manuals are modified to specifically address the needs of our participants (that is, women); and the themes of the workshops also are modified to focus on needs that may be stronger for women than for men: abuse issues, co-dependent relationships, dysfunctional family dynamics, anger control issues, self-harm and substance abuse, etc.

Lead Facilitators come from diverse professional careers: psychologists, scientists, educators and corporate trainers, all of whom volunteer with the Peace Between People Organization of Seattle, Washington, which sponsors AVP. The collaborative training efforts of these volunteers have enabled me to use my own creativity to be useful in our workshops, and to mentor other Leads.

To prepare for this work, to train myself as a lecturer and facilitator within and outside of my work with AVP, I studied the findings of many prominent behavioral psychologists and other researchers (a partial list is offered as an appendix) in fields relating to the after-effects of abuse and trauma, group dynamics, etc. Some of the more established works are mentioned below, but there are many more. I have also read theoretical propositions, methodologies, and experimental design formats used to conduct such research. To broaden my knowledge, I have sought out contradictory as well as supportive follow-up research findings. I continue to keep abreast of any recent applications or citations of related studies to update or modify my work.

Participants in this institutional setting are often seeking "self-awareness and self-esteem building," and "intellectual and emotional insight." Therefore, these topics have been woven into my presentations as well.

"Being totally involved in numerous programs definitely contributed to my growth, my spirituality; programs such as AVP, Life Skills, Domestic Violence, C.D., MRT, and adult Basic education helped to give me a sense of self worth and value." (C56).

The American Psychological Association's guidelines are incorporated into each AVP opening talk. These guidelines are a part of any volunteer work I do, as they provide a sound foundation for work that entails personal, intimate disclosure and psychosocial involvement.

The APA guidelines as used in AVP, and now Peace Talks, are:

1) Written request to join the program. (AVP participation requires all participants to personally express, in writing, their desire to attend a workshop. It is not permitted to send someone to participate on a mandatory basis.)

2) Informed consent.

3) Freedom to withdraw participation.

4) Debriefings and protection from harm.

5) Confidentiality.

We also have a special rule that makes all the difference, in a prison setting. In a departure from the prison's normal requirements for security, during an AVP workshop staff does not interrupt an inmate — or, if they do, it is done as discreetly as possible.

To understand some of the theory behind the design of our overall program and the components within it, consider Sperry and Gazzaniga's work on the "split brain." Their research has been extensive and their findings are rarely questioned. They have established that specialized functions exist in the right hemisphere of the brain (i.e., facial recognition, problem solving with spatial relationships), distinct from the specialized functions of the left hemisphere (which is the primary center for language, i.e., speaking, writing, reading, and mathematical calculations).

Gazzaniga (1985) has also theorized that, in some cases, a person with an undisturbed *corpus callosum* (in other words, with a normal, intact brain) may still experience incomplete communication between left and right hemispheres. One result could be that emotional information may be shut out of the left hemisphere so that it is not stored in the usual language format, leaving a person uncertain about her emotions and unable to communicate verbally why she feels the way she does. This may incline that individual to create a wrong explanation for her feelings, as the left hemisphere attempts to compensate for the missing data that is held only in the right hemisphere. When feelings are misinterpreted, the results can be dramatic. We try to bear in mind this possibility when working with participants.

This field has been the focus of study for over two decades and it caught the interest of University of Chicago psycho-biologist, Jarre Levy. Levy asserts that we should seek to "integrate" this gloriously differentiated brain to heighten our overall intelligence and abilities, drawing from each hemisphere's specialized resources.

In seeking to expand the areas of self-awareness to cover life events that are not generally broached in group therapy, or "one-on-one" type counseling, we select educational and emotionally-provocative exercises. To achieve this end, standard AVP exercises are implemented or invented that are specifically tailored to tap into these hidden areas of hemisphere non-communication.

One such exercise is called "Tinker-Toy Construction." This is a non-verbal activity where the participants build things, using Tinker Toys, to illustrate an emotion or idea. Themes like anger, or freedom, might be included. While the construction is being built, the others in the group must silently give up the vision they have, and find a way to allow a collaboration to occur. This can be very trying and can prompt uncomfortable memories and emotions.

As the exercise progresses, the participant is often stimulated by recollections and associations attached to the action. These prime her for the other exercises, which allow emotional catharsis as the workshop agenda progresses. Psychological barriers are broken by this systematic method of mixing non-verbal, kinetic and emotional recall into the workshop format.

Trust exercises are used, as well. They require a participant to close her eyes while others guide her around the room; lift her body off the ground; and move her from one participant to another.

Due to the disclosure and personal revelation our participants' experience, group and individual debriefs are an important part of the closing of each exercise and session.

In preparation, prior to each workshop, the facilitators and Lead conduct pre-planning sessions. They review list of participants, searching for potentially problematic combinations (certain inmates are known to consider each other enemies or have other problems together), they consider the mental health concerns of participants, and so on. Careful attention is paid to the individual aspects of each participant. Unlike the professional mental health workers or other counselors that may be brought in from "outside," peer facilitators have an inside line on the participants, as they share the same environment.

Two Lead Facilitators generally oversee the work of an apprentice facilitator and a number of full facilitators. Not all facilitators reach Lead status. To be a candidate for promotion to Lead, intuitive abilities are required, as well as leadership qualities, and advanced mastery of the group processes and the exercises covered in the manuals for at the Basic and advanced program levels plus the material presented in a special Training for Trainers. Experience as a Facilitator, and the votes of other Leads, also count. No workshop can be conducted without at least one registered Lead Facilitator.

After the team of facilitators has gone over the list of participants, the exercises to be incorporated into the agenda are then chosen by those who wish to facilitate them. The Leads will address any concerns about the level of experience needed to conduct the more advanced exercises. Next, each facilitator is encouraged to identify her strengths and weaknesses in presenting the upcoming workshop, and she is given the opportunity to state what she would like in terms of support in handling these areas. Once these particulars have been completed, each facilitator is responsible for preparing for the assigned exercises.

The Basic, Advanced, and Training For Trainers workshops are each a 3-day commitment. The three days generally are comprised of nine sessions, each running about 2 ½ hours (3 sessions per day). A standard Basic Workshop incorporates several specific exercises which will be given in a set sequence, so that each one builds on the previous one.

The Basic Workshop

A participant begins in a Basic three-day workshop. There, the participant remains in an area segregated from non-attending inmates, usually a classroom. Each day begins at 8:00 AM and ends at 4:00 PM. This segregating of participants from non-participants helps reduce outside distractions and builds a sense of community, which is essential when it comes to the trust exercises and personal disclosures, and the catharsis and emotional expression that the workshop provokes.

There are four basic elements in a workshop format that remain stable, because they work. The process is the power, as they say.

These are the principles of non-violent action:

1) Affirmation
2) Community Building
3) Communication Skills
4) Conflict Resolution

The Basic agenda introduces the elements of personal change. This concept is termed "Transforming Power." Exercises in the Basic workshop allow the participants to learn experientially. The processes become active as the exercises engage the participant in two ways, implicitly and explicitly.

An example of a first-session agenda facilitators would construct in their pre-planning meeting follows. All agendas are posted and noted prior to a session's beginning.

The Opening Talk

The session begins with an explanation of how AVP began, and a discussion of its purpose of conducting conflict resolution skills: All participants and facilitators are volunteers, all shared information is confidential. Everyone is important and valuable. AVP's philosophy is "Transforming Power." The workshop is based on participant experience, it is not a rap session or therapy. One objective is to develop a sense of community in the group, based on respect for all the people in it. The workshop's basic goal is for the participants to develop their own power; and, especially, to discover non-violent ways to deal with conflict. Requirements are to remain open, to look at and talk about conflict while affirming each person, using communication and cooperation skills to create positive conflict resolutions.

Conflicts which participants have played a part in are shared, and then the group creatively explores potential solutions. Together, the participants seek alternative perspectives while identifying the behaviors that increase or decrease violence.

To create a safe community and build trust, ground rules are introduced. These are written on poster paper and remain posted.

AVP Ground Rules

1. We look to affirm one another's good points.
2. We refrain from put-downs, of ourselves and others.
3. We listen to what each person has to say; we do not interrupt each other and we don't speak too often or too long. Shy people: Don't be afraid to speak up; we need your contribution. Talkative people: Have your say, but do not monopolize the conversation.
4. When volunteering, volunteer yourself only. Don't volunteer other people.
5. We observe confidentiality regarding the personal sharing of each participant. Nothing that is said here is to be repeated outside this workshop.
6. Everyone has the right to pass; participation in every component of the program is voluntary.

The facilitator asks the group to raise their hands if they accept these rules, and if they will follow them. After agreement is established, several points are explained in greater detail.

- The subject matter presented is intended to serve the needs of the group. At the end of each session, all participants will evaluate the exercise and express what was good or not good for them. Their comments are written beside the posted Agenda Session Outline.
- Games called "Light-and-Livelies" are explained. While seeming silly, they inject a sense of fun, raising energies and helping everyone relax.
- Attendance is expected at every session, once the program has begun, to maintain the community building.
- "Clinicing" is when facilitators need to separate themselves from the group to talk, resolve questions and determine how to best serve individual and group needs as they emerge.
- Unanswered questions, which may come up for participants, can be written on the blank sheet posted.
- Housekeeping details, smoking breaks and other miscellaneous issues are gone over.

The intrinsic quality of the given session emerges predictably, but every time the exercises are conducted, it is a unique experience. Each group of participants brings different memories and different strengths and weaknesses that influence the process and the outcome.

The session begins with the opening talk, then an agenda review identifying who will facilitate which portions. As the introduction of the team proceeds, each facilitator says why she is in AVP. My own introduction would be along the lines of this:

> I've tried all kinds of ways to find balance and happiness in my life, through drugs, sex, distractions, but never got that inner 'fix' to stay. I found that my hardships made me hard like a shell or wall, that kept life out. AVP breaks me free of that self-imprisonment. I want healthy relationships where I don't have to worry that the person next to me is going to tell me he's going to kill me this morning or I have to help him do a crime — I want to work for a living in such a way that the system can't come back at me and tell me they're "taking it all, because it's criminal profit." I want to be a good mom, so that my child can see how I live, and the choices I make, and not worry that they'll take me away again. I want to be a role model for others so they can make healthy choices and find fulfillment inside. I choose to love, I choose to be at peace with the world. AVP is the only program I've found that guides me, teaches me and allows me to take those steps to change. It's changed my life, but first I had to choose to allow it. What I want to get out of this workshop is more of that, and to help the rest of you experience what I'm talking about.

[In addition to helping to frame the upcoming experience for other participants, this little speech models honest and personal disclosure, which helps them trust me and know that they are safe to open up in similar ways.]

Each participant then is asked to answer, in one sentence, why she is attending the workshop and what she wants to get out of it.

The first game or exercise is selected to help the group members gain insight into their fellow participants. Each woman is asked to create an adjective name. It must be affirming and positive: "Learning Lynn." The adjective can be a trait that the participant desires, but has not yet realized. Each participant must repeat the names that came prior to her own, which at first may be seen as nothing but a little game to test one's memory but which really helps develop eye contact among participants and build intimacy: Learning Lynn, Kind Katie, Happy Heidi, Smart Suzi . . ."

The second exercise is "Affirmation in Two's." The participants are paired up randomly, by counting off, and given two minutes to speak. They are to say only positive things about themselves. As one talks, the other listens, making eye contact but with no verbal input — only facial expressions or nods. After two minutes, the roles are reversed. That done, each one of the pair must introduce her partner to the pair beside them, repeating the positive things the speaker revealed about herself. In the process, each participant hears herself spoken about positively, in front of other people. Even under this artificial construct, this can be a surprisingly emotional experience.

Now, the first "processing" of an exercise begins. In this instance, each participant states what that experience was like for her. Routine responses are these:

"I never say anything positive about myself, so I couldn't' think of anything much at first."

"I felt embarrassed."

"It was hard to just sit and not say anything to my partner about what she was saying."

"It was great to have someone actually listen to me; I never had that happen before."

"It was awesome to hear another person say good things about me."

A "light and lively" is then introduced. One game is like musical chairs, where one person stands in the center and says "The Big Wind Blows for anyone who . . . has children [or anything else about herself, or what she is wearing]." Everyone whom that statement applies to must switch chairs with someone else. The person left without a chair then stands in the center. This is still building on personal disclosure, yet allows kinetic activity and laughter, relieving some of the stress that accumulates.

Then brainstorming begins, with a discussion on "what is violence." Participants are asked to help write responses on large poster paper for all to see. "Drugs, abuse, lies, punching, war, guns, poverty, racism, sexism, unfairness," are typically brought forth as participants respond.

Next the participants are asked to talk about their ideas on the causes of violence: "Hatred, greed, power, pain, fear." This may all be summarized, then, into a paragraph. One example is, "From this brainstorming session, the *causes* are what produce the violent response, the response comes *second*. Now, this applies to anger also. *Anger is a secondary emotion.* Next time you get angry, ask yourself, "Where is all this coming form?" Fear, loss, what? Am I angry at so and so because she said something that hurt my feelings? Why did it hurt me? Am I afraid she no longer likes me, so that hurts, because I like her liking me? It feels good to be liked. So do I use anger to hurt her back? Next, ask yourself, "By hurting her in retaliation, will I get my wishes met? My real desire is that she truly likes me, because it feels good!"

All this is fit into 2 ½ hours. The evaluation of the exercise begins, and every response is written beside the exercise on the agenda. The closing exercise is short, and it is just called "closing" (not "exercise"), although this too is part of the process. A closing may be: "Everyone stand, I'll put my hand out first and say how I feel right now, then anyone join in, put your hand on top of mine and say a word or two about how you feel now." "Relaxed," "Cautious," "Excited . . ."

This sample of a session helps to demonstrate the beginning of a formula which will be replicated, over and over, in the subsequent sessions. As the sessions evolve, so does the intensity of each subsequent exercise's focus; this is responded to emotionally by the participants.

The Eight Main Sessions

Activities used during the sessions that follow the Opening include:

Concentric Circles. Half of the group sits in an outer circle, the other half are seated facing them. The facilitator asks questions of those in the outer circle, who will answer to the inner circle partners in front of them. Questions vary, and if standard ones are not particularly appropriate, a Lead will help to structure the question to insure that it works as it should. This is timed so that after the outer circle responds, the inner circle will also answer.

Here are some questions (created for use in an Advanced or T4T workshop, not a Basic):

A time when I was confused, and I could barely cope, was ___.
When I've experienced violence against me, I felt ___, because ___.

A series of such questions builds a momentum of sorts, which stimulates memories and provokes emotional reactions. The focus is on the participants' feelings and allowing them to express them openly. Demonstrations of compassion and sympathy can be given by a hug, or a shared secret — different groups bring different responses, as do different questions. Questions are issued by the facilitator to keep the interaction going. Questions are directed to the entire group; no one is singled out. (These are open-ended questions, like: "Why were you triggered and how did it feel?") In an open group discussion, whoever chooses to answer does.

Exercises like this one do stimulate the emotions and stir vivid memories; this means that a safe processing-out must be provided before sending the participants on their way. This processing-out aids in the integration of the experience with the concepts. By sharing their experience with the group and having the group respond to their comments, participants may gain new perspectives, validation, and the realization of commonality with others.

Because this can lead to some in-depth and valuable sharing, during the processing-out of an exercise we are less concerned with keeping a strict watch on time. This deviation in the session planning is expected and is taken into account by the facilitators in every workshop. While certain elements exist that cannot be sacrificed, such as particular exercises that embody required elements, there are the other exercises which can be eliminated or shortened. There is an art in judging where and how to trim the agenda, which requires a well-seasoned facilitator or Lead.

Skills in listening and speaking with "I" statements are essential and cannot be cut. Role-plays are very popular. There are several forms in which these can be conducted. Scenarios can be pre-determined, created in advance for the specific level of audience. Prior to a role-play, other groundwork will have begun to set up skills and insight into handling conflicts. Empathy exercises, such as "In common," offer the opportunity for the participants to discover many common likes and dislikes they share with each other. Teams are created, and on a tight time limitation they try to find points they all agree on: We like chocolate, have kids, believe in God, don't like math, lived in a city, like to cook, like the beach . . . This exercise helps women to see that there are similarities among them and it reduces their sense of aloneness or separateness from others of different backgrounds. Empathy is born when they begin to relate to one another.

Transforming Power (TP), the heart of the AVP message, is explained. Transforming Power is that power within which is true goodness, stemming from altruistically motivated love. It is the force for peace and fairness that can drive one on, through life's most challenging conflicts and choices, seemingly exhaustible. Examples are Martin Luther King Jr., Gandhi, Jesus and countless mothers who have overcome obstacles and survived disasters that could have destroyed them, but they were miraculously driven to defend and care for their children — and so, they survive. Each individual defines Transforming Power in her own terms, but it resides in the soul of all humans and is available if we choose to access it.

Its principles cover:
- Resolving conflicts and reaching a friendly understanding,
- Entering conflict with the belief that each person has a part of him or her that wants to do what is right. That "right," within, is constantly sought.
- Putting oneself in the other's shoes, seeking to discover and understand why other people act and feel the way they do.

- Constant re-examination of oneself and the position one plays in a conflict: Is it honest, fair and considerate of others?

After TP is introduced, at some point a "TP rap" will be given to the group by a facilitator. The "rap" is usually an incident in which TP was successfully used — a short story of personal struggle, in which the decision was made to use TP, and with it the struggle was transformed.

A role-play scenario presents a conflict between two people. Difficult situations that a participant may not know how to confront can be used as subject matter. The first scene depicts the actual reality. The scene played after is a repeat, only with one character using Transforming Power. Typically, these "games" provoke many emotions in the players and require in-depth debriefing. Then the role-plays are picked apart to determine their components and what caused the situation to escalate — and when, precisely, did it *de*-escalate and why? Participants identify the turning point in which Transforming Power began to be felt, and assess whether the situation ended in a win-win situation.

The AVP workshops are unquestionably the most popular activity within the prison for inter-personal and social growth. Waiting lists have extended beyond the 1-year mark. As in POCAAN peer educating, the facilitators serve their peers beyond the workshops. Paperwork is also a duty, which includes distributing and gathering questionnaires for attending participants [these are passed out on the close of the third day of each workshop]. After everyone has left, the questionnaires are read and shared by the facilitator team. Comments are reviewed in the facilitators' debriefing so that future sessions can be improved; and the accumulated data is kept on file in the Peace Between People Office Seattle.

To the question, "What changes would you like to see in the workshop?" by far the most frequent response is that "It was not long enough! I love it."

Those of us who have served as facilitators for many workshops are aware that the women in prison yearn for opportunities to learn and develop interpersonal skills and social connecting. The thing I have found most wanting in the prison environment is the lack of opportunities to express love and maintain healthy relationships. AVP is unique in that it seeks to promote kindness, empathy, and gentle expressions of compassion; all of these speak to the souls of women.

And in prison, we are dealing with many women who have been separated from their babies, who may have lost custodial rights over their children (under certain legislative decrees, a mother forfeits parental rights based on the length of her imprisonment — 36+ months). One suffering mother writes,

> "I strangled the man who molested my children and I don't care what anybody thinks about me because I know who I am and what I stand for!!! The superintendent denied my right to have trailer visits [family visits allowed, as a privilege, in a slightly more home-like setting] with my oldest daughter because my crime was considered domestic violence due to the fact that it was my daughter's father who was strangled to death in my crime even tho we were never married. So my answer is more personal contact like trailer visits with my oldest daughter. Two hours in the visiting room is not enough, especially when I have 5 more years of incarceration left." (AI9)

Workshops are offered as often as they can be run, practically speaking. The schedule calls for one a month; however, because an outside Lead has to invest six very full days in preparing and conducting each workshop, many factors interfere, not least of them work obligations. Remember, all facilitators are volunteers, unlike the POCAAN positions which are paid for by grants.

During my five-year involvement with AVP, I have facilitated and/or assisted in approximately 30 workshops. I calculate that each one requires three 12-hour days performing my duties as a facilitator (that is, 36 hours in each workshop); additional pre-planning work and time spent coordinating internal logistics and team-related responsibilities add up to 10 hours per workshop. At 46 hours per workshop, this means I have been immersed in this work for a total of *1,380 hours*, from 1996 to 2000 alone.

Should I mention the additional 3 hours per month devoted to facilitator meetings, and 2 hours for leading the participant support group (that estimate takes into account those workshops that were canceled)? That means an additional 240 hours 1996 through 2000, for a combined total of 1620 hours of AVP duty and participation.

During these four years, a total of 800 women attended the workshops and support group activities.

Workshops with women always bring out the emotional gamut a woman experiences. It is not uncommon to see five or ten of the 130 participants crying over an experience one of the others has shared, or triggered by an exercise, or the story of another woman. The delicate balance of trust and sense of community creates an environment in which empathy can be born and flourish. The reactions are profound. I have never witnessed a more powerful or constructive approach of personal expression/emotion coupled educationally for cognitive development. What we call "rehabilitation" can only be realized if new attitudes, behaviors, ideas and emotional health are created within the individual. AVP has met the requisite conditions.

These are some of the starting points by which AVP helps participants gain perspective on their life experiences.

6. A relationship in which I had to be perfect was ___.

7. A time I was not allowed to show or express my anger was ___.

8. When I stayed in an abusive relationship, it was because ___.

9. A time when I was told to be someone I really wasn't was ___.

10. When I don't express my true feelings, I sometimes do these behaviors ___.

11. I would describe a co-dependent person as someone who ___.

12. If someone wanted to stop being a co-dependent person, I think they should start by ___.

13. It's important for me to be open and able to express my ideas and feelings because ___.

14. I can encourage others to be open and honest with me by ___.

In the course of the program, participants asked certain types of questions with outstanding frequency and these signs of concern influenced what material we selected to teach to the groups. Even excluding those questions specific to STDs, the women's questions showed that they were abysmally ignorant about their own bodies and a woman's normal sexuality, and about normal human relations in general. Some of the most common questions were:

- What is abuse?
- What is normal in a woman's body: how should the genitalia look, what's the normal size of labia, or vagina; where are the urethra, cervix, ovaries; what discharges are common throughout the menstrual cycle?
- What is normal in female sexuality?
- What are "boundaries"?
- How do you get self-esteem?
- What are human rights?

POCAAN's services utilize the peers of the targeted group to provide education because only peers can effectively communicate and gain access within the closed and often secret worlds of prisoners. A peer has knowledge of the unspoken rules and ability to break down medical terminology into a language they can understand.

A preface to the presentation might be: "I don't want to offend anyone, so be prepared that I am going to use somewhat crude language. I'm going to be talking about life and death, and I want to be sure every woman here understands everything I say, Okay?"

For example, we would not get very far by explaining that "Pre-semen secretion from a male's penis, prior to ejaculation, is found to contain higher levels of HIV than actual semen. Precautions should be implemented prior to any bodily contact."

Translated into "street" language during a presentation, it would run something like this:

> You know that see-through stuff, pre-cum? It's like concentrated HIV. If you think, Oh it's cool, I'll just get him started, but I won't let him finish in my mouth; it'll be okay," you are wrong, sister, cause check this out, if you cut your lip, from the pipe, you know what I'm talking about — you smoke so much Rock, your lips crack. That crack opens up your body to take in any virus or germ it comes into contact with, and it can get in your blood stream and then, well, if it's the HIV from some trick or your man or your woman . . . you just got infected.
>
> Or, how about if you just let him rub his stuff between your legs, those lips down there? All that tender skin is mucus membrane, just like the inside of your mouth, nose and eyes, and it's like a human sponge. Whatever you put on it can get sucked right up into your bloodstream; all it needs is to have a little tear in it, that you may not know is there or feel. See, women are like that, we have all that human sponge between our legs that men don't have. Only the head of their cocks are mucus membrane, the base and balls are tougher skin, like the top of your hand. Think, too, about how they shoot everything out of their body; we don't. Our bodies are the receivers, things go up into our insides, that's how we get pregnant. If you had one guy with HIV, and he f—ed or got a blow job from 10 different women without using safer sex protection, how many women would catch the virus from him? Probably 8, so let's say one of those girls who are now infected goes and gives blow jobs and or f—s 10 uninfected men, without protection. How many men do you think would catch the virus from one girl? Maybe one, because they shoot it out and it cleans the pipe, so to speak.

At this point, I would do a demonstration to show how to pinch the tip of the condom and carefully roll it down. "Well, you're thinking 'that's cool, if the dude lets you,' but what if he says: 'no way'?" I then have the participants volunteer to show me, in a role-play. Invariably, they show a resistant, resentful partner or a dominating one that orders them through force (violence) to stop, and tells them to shut up and just open their legs. Then, I address how we are each given rights, just because we were born, "Human rights, that say we have the right to make decisions over our own body and to be treated with respect.

What we feel, and what we think, are real and important to us, and if anyone refuses to treat our feelings and thoughts with understanding and respect, then it becomes our responsibility to get out of that relationship. We can't make anyone change, only ourselves."

These points would then be more fully explained. A handout on Human Rights would be distributed. I would ask for more volunteers to repeat what the last role-play expressed, this time modeling assertiveness and the beliefs outlined in the Human Rights list as their response to the victimization. I would then repeat the role of the victim, myself, changing my words and behavior to deal with the situation.

> Bottom line, it's going to be you who has to leave the situation. That's what it can come to. Battered women's shelters are there if you look for them. I know, because I was one of the women that took the beatings and was stitched up and X-rayed in emergency rooms. I was the one who lied to protect my abuser, because I thought he'd kill me. I ran from the truth, covered my fears with prescription drugs. Till one day, with my newborn in my arms and just the clothes on my back, I ran away . . . selling my body for food and shelter was safer for us than staying. We didn't have shelters, then.

The scene then would be modeled with the victim using her knowledge of her rights and assertiveness skills. I would then recruit other volunteer participants, allowing as many women as possible to role-play, using assertiveness skills. The passive women rarely volunteered at the beginning of a role play, but over time they joined in. For the rest of the audience, the repetition helped reinforce the lesson so they might remember it when they needed it.

Other safer sex practices were also taught. For one, we used the artificial penis to practice condom application while performing oral sex on a man. A participant would hold model the role of the man — this invariably brought much laughter and incidentally served to relax the group. As the role-play began, the demonstrator would show how one could covertly remove a condom from a pocket, place it in one's mouth and, while performing oral sex, put the condom in place. We also taught them to incorporate latex gloves in their relations; these were introduced as part of a sexual fantasy, explaining to the partner, "It's a doctor thing." This story gave the woman a good excuse for taking a close look at her sex-partner's body while she was, in fact, checking for signs of a sexually transmitted disease.

Lectures

Presenting lectures is one of the strategies by which program facilitators can assist the participants in comprehending different views of reality and other ways of looking at a situation. Concepts are presented in simple language, as modeled below.

Key Elements of Lecture Content

- Boundaries

Every person has the right to be treated with respect and dignity. Your boundaries are also your right. A boundary is a rule you create that protects your comfort zone. There are boundaries you decide on, such as: how close you like a stranger to stand next to you; how sexual you want to be with someone; whether or not you trust a person enough to lend money; sharing personal secrets; having privacy to change your clothes; in short, your boundaries are the laws you make up to maintain the safety of that country you call your life.

- Co-dependency

People can be addicted to many things, from alcohol to relationships. Co-dependency is described in different ways by different people, but its bottom line is that a person doesn't feel complete or free from terror unless they are with their significant other. It doesn't matter that the significant other beats them, because — as scary as it is to be with them — it's scarier to be alone. Then too, co-dependency may not involve physical violence; it may be an emotional, psychological, behavioral condition, a response to living under oppressive rules which don't allow open expression or talk about one's feelings or problems. Co-dependency is an addictive process.

- Abuse

There are many forms of abuse, which range from physical to emotional, psychological, and spiritual. Physical abuse includes shoving, slapping, biting, hitting one another; all of these are violence. Destroying someone's personal property is also a tactic used in abuse; so is denial of food or necessities. Emotional abuse can be as subtle as not talking, or ignoring another, as though they were less than human, or incompetent. Psychological abuse somewhat ties in with emotional abuse. A man who tells his wife that he is going to kill her children if she tries to leave him can terrorize a victim into not leaving a dangerous situation, which, in turn causes an emotional response. If a victim is lied to about being unattractive, she may come to believe that no one but the abuser will take her. Similarly, if she is told that her perceptions are always wrong, she may begin to believe she is incapable of forming logical thoughts or conclusions about the world around her. Sexism and gender biases, racism, and classism may also show up as forms of psychological abuse. Spiritual abuse can be found in some cults, and, like emotional abuse, is related to lies relatiing to psychological abuse. One prevalent issue is sex; "It's a sin to refuse your husband sex"; "You will go to hell if you are a homosexual," and so forth.

- Sexual Abuse

This form of abuse is overtly recognized in rape cases; however, rape is not often recognized when it occurs. Rape occurs when a woman says 'no' but her partner forces her to go forward with the sexual activity. Often, because she did agree to kiss and fondle, she may believe it was her fault when her date refused to stop at the fondling stage and proceeded to physically overpower her and do further sexual acts she did not want. Demanding that someone participate in degrading sex acts and humiliating games involving sex can all constitute sexual abuse.

- Self-Esteem Building

To esteem oneself is to respect oneself. This is not the same as thinking you are better looking or smarter than someone else. Self esteem is something a woman gives herself; it is part of her personal friendship with herself; a form of self-love. The choices we make in each interaction with ourselves and others are ways we can build or hurt our self-esteem. Respecting and honoring our own values and expressing our own truths are healthy expressions of self esteem. Being able to admit mistakes and a willingness to grow and learn are also ways we self-love. Self esteem is a right every human being is entitled to enjoy.

- Communication Skills

To have better relationships and to meet our needs and desires, good communication skills are very important. Each person has hidden filters in the mind which alter perceptions from one person to the next. These filters were made by our past experiences, culture, beliefs, values, assumptions, expectations, self-esteem, and prejudices. If a woman has low self-esteem and someone tells her she is smart, she may pass that information through her filters and think the compliment was a smart-ass remark, really intended to put her down. She may, in turn, lash out and tell the friendly person something cruel to hurt their feelings because in her mind, the compliment was really an insult.

Communication is more than the words we say. It is what we think and what we do in our actions. If a parent strikes a child but says, "I love you," the parent is communicating more than what is being spoken. And what one word may mean to you may mean something entirely different to someone else. The term "bitch" is, to some, a female dog, or a sexist insult; other people use it to indicate a hard task or punishment.

Body language is another form of communication. Posture, eye contact, facial expressions can all say things to the listener that can help or hurt you in successfully communicating what you mean.

Sometimes, a carefully made "I" statement can be a useful tool to express your feelings about what someone is doing. The sentence can be broken into three parts: "When ____, I feel ____, because____. First you identify the behavior that you want to talk about; second, you accurately disclose your main feeling; third, you clarify what it does to you — the tangible effect on your life.

Listening is perhaps the most difficult of communication skills. Listening is really an art and is something most of us could improve on. Just think of the problems created in your life from others misinterpreting what you said. Just as your words or actions have been inaccurately interpreted, have you misinterpreted others' intentions?

Good listening is called "active listening," because you must be actively engaged and focused on the person speaking to you. Active listeners use body language to affirm that the speaker has their attention; they wait to ask clarifying questions (also known as rephrasing the speaker's words) to make sure that the listener is grasping the true intent of the speaker; they admit any difficulties in understanding the speaker's point and ask for more information about the issue; they phrase any conflict in question form, not as an accusation; they work to keep an open mind and make notes of things to be remembered.

Structure of Lecture Sessions

We do all we can to build in gradual steps, presenting the information in ways the women can understand and use. We use the common language level of the women to share concepts that are often presented in arcane academic terms; these topics can be simplified to reach an uneducated but needy audience.

The "talking head" portion of the session is kept pretty short, and is followed by interactive exercises. During lectures we also use flip charts to write down the key ideas of the lecture's content. Ad lib role-playing may be incorporated, to allow the audience to act out a scene depicting the action being discussed. Other techniques that have helped participants absorb the lessons, and open up their own range of expression, include:

- Assigned pairing with another participant to discuss an example of the subject, as they have personally experienced it in their own life. This activity is timed, to make sure that each participant has a chance to speak.
- Open-group dialogue to express what they learned or to ask clarifying questions.
- Optional one-on-one talks with a facilitator.
- Writing assignments similar to journal writings.
- Collage construction, assembling pre-cut magazine photos to express visually the participants' feelings or hopes.
- Drawing, painting, charcoal and pastel.
- Writing personal poetry.

Workshops include learning-game activities relating to each subject under discussion.

7. Trouble in TEC

The TEC (Treatment Evaluation Center), the re-named Special Needs Unit (SNU), is WCCW's mental ward. As such, it is a maximum-security area. It had, and has, a restricted-access population. Inmates not housed in TEC wards are unable to talk with the inmates housed in TEC, unless by way of a chance meeting in the medical clinic; then, two inmates might briefly exchange a few covert words. The information which began to emerge, first in the mid-1980s and then again in the mid-1990s, was alarming, especially in regard to the housing conditions and treatment of inmates.

Power over Our Own Life

In order to appreciate some of the psychological dynamics of the situation, in addition to the obvious mental and physical punishment that was (perhaps in some cases not entirely intentionally) being administered, we should digress briefly to look at a field experiment that was conducted by Langer and Rodin in an institutional setting, in 1976.[1] The study examined the effects of the psychological concept of control.

Langer and Rodin concluded that how much you control possess (and how much you don't) can prove to be the most important determinant of any human

---

1. Langer, E-J, and Rodin, J. 1976. *Journal of Personality and Social Psychology*, 34, 191-198. Cited in Hock, R., (1999) *Forty Studies that Changed Psychology.*

behavior. Your personal power, your sense of competence help define your options in life. If your sense of personal power is reduced, your choices will be reduced correspondingly. Control (in your living environment, your life and the events in it, not other people or their actions!) produces feelings which shape your perceptions of what you can and cannot do. What you recognize to be available to you as choices are reflections of your personal sense of power; and your behavior is dictated by the choices you perceive you actually have.

If your perceptions say these choices are being threatened, you'll experience negative feelings and will combat this infringement on your personal power, by behaving in ways that seek to restore it. *Reactance* is the term used to indicate this tendency to resist any infringement that is liable to limit one's freedom.

When control over your own life and environment are taken away from you, and you cannot get it back, the psychological conflict can give rise to a sense of helplessness.[2] Anxiety, anger, depression, outrage, and physical illness or a weakened immune system are possible collateral effects. Many studies have illustrated that stressful situations can cause a wide range of negative effects on people; yet, if these same people are given a belief that they can make a difference to the stressful event and claim some control over it, the negative effects will be reduced — just because they believe some of their control has been restored. A crowded elevator provided a funny illustration of this principle. A study in 1978 found that when a person is standing next to the control panel in a crowded elevator, she will perceive that there are fewer people in it than people standing in other positions throughout the car will think — only because she has a greater sense of control within the given environment.[3]

A similar study expands upon the point. Two groups of people were exposed to loud bursts of noise, while they were supposed to be finding the solutions to various problem-solving tasks. One group of subjects had no control over the bursts of noise. The other group was informed that, by pressing a button, they could avoid the blast of noise. However, this "control-button" group was requested to *not* press the button, if at all possible. The "no-button" group performed the problem-solving tasks significantly less successfully than the "control-button" group. Interestingly, the "button of control" group endured all

---

2.This recalls Seligman's experiments on learned helplessness, using dogs as test cases. A brief description is available online: Dr. Beverly Potter, 2002. Loss of Control & Burnout, in *Overcoming Job Burnout — Self-Paced Instruction* at http://www.docpotter.com/boclass-0toc.html [Cited August 1, 2002], from *Overcoming Job Burnout: How to Renew Enthusiasm for Work*, Dr. Beverly Potter. Berkeley, California: Ronin Publishing, 2002.

3. Rodin, Solomon and Metcalf, 1978

the bursts of noise, just as the no-button group. They never did push the button. Still, they scored higher. Why? Because that choice "to push the button or not" gave them a sense of control.

The power to choose gives us a more confident outlook and a greater sense of effectiveness in the world. Old age, physical handicaps, incarceration can all transform our lives into option-less realities. When circumstance places people in an environment such as a nursing home or retirement home, new illnesses follow. Heart disease, colitis and depression are among those diseases associated with feelings of helplessness and loss of control.

Langer and Rodin proposed the theory that, as personal responsibility is lost and an individual's ability to control her environment is taken away, her sense power and happiness also diminishes. Therefore, giving power back to such people ought to reverse this tendency, and their responses should likewise be measurably improved. Enhanced mental acuity, physical activity and satisfaction with life should be apparent in the subjects' behavior and attitudes, and enhanced health and a stronger immune system should be apparent as signs of improvement.

To test out their theory (derived from their previous work and others), the two obtained the cooperation of Arden House, a nursing home in Connecticut, to use their residents as a test population. If the scientists could improve their patients' sense of well being, why not? Rated as one of the best nursing homes by the state, Arden House offered quality medical care, recreational facilities and fine residential conditions. Four large residential units housed a fairly homogeneous population whose socioeconomic backgrounds were similar and whose physical and psychological conditions were comparable.

When each new resident arrived, a room would be assigned according to availability. On average, the floors were equivalent. For this study, two floors were randomly selected to test two experimental "treatment" conditions. The fourth-floor residents, 8 men and 39 women, received "increased-responsibility" treatments. The second floor, 9 men and 35 women, was designated as the comparison group. These 91 subjects ranged in ages 65 to 90.

The procedure was set in place with the administrator. The administrator was a friendly, outgoing 33-year-old who had daily interactions with his residents. Calling a meeting with the two floors, he explained he had new information to give them about Arden House. He gave each group a separate, though similar, statement. On the fourth floor, he informed the "responsibility-induced" group: "You have the responsibility of caring for yourselves and determining your own activities regarding: a) the arrangement of furnishings in your room, with or without staff assistance), b) making your complaints known and letting us know what changes you desire, c) selecting a personal plant from the Arden gift tray. If you choose to take one, these plants are your own to keep and care for as you choose, d) selecting a night, Thursday or Friday, to watch a movie or to not watch it. And, e) Arden House desires to make your lives as comfortable and pleasant as possible.

Normally, Arden House residents were allowed to make these choices anyway; for the purposes of this experiment, that policy was merely reiterated and clarified to the people on the fourth floor.

By contrast, the comparison group on the second floor was told that Arden House wanted to make their lives fuller and more interesting. The emphasis was not on "you" but "we." We want your rooms to look nice . . . we've tried to make them comfortable . . . we want you to be happy . . . we feel it's our responsibility . . . I give you . . . The nurse would not let them select their own plant, either. Here the nurse selected the plant and gave it to them. And, "We're showing a movie . . . we'll let you know when you are scheduled to see it." Three days later, the director repeated the messages to each resident room. Thus, the "responsibility-induced" residents were given the enhanced impression that they could exercise some control over their lives in a variety of ways, superficial as they might be. The second floor residents were told that [even these] decisions were being made for them. These policies were enforced for a three-week duration.

Would the perception of having increased responsibility cause a reaction? One week prior to the administrator's talk to each group, each person in the test population responded to a questionnaire. Three weeks later, the experiment now complete, the questionnaire was answered again. Its contents related to the amount of control the residents felt they had, how happy they were and how active they were at home.

The second questionnaire was given to the nurses on each floor, all of whom had no knowledge of the experiment. Each nurse was asked to rate patients on 10-point scales regarding the following issues: how happy the resident appeared, how alert, independent, sociable, active; and sleeping and eating habits. Two records of the residents' behavior were kept: measurements of movie attendance and participation in a contest (residents could write their guess about how many beans were in a jar of jelly beans).

The results of these two questionnaires showed marked differences, which validated the researchers' presumption of the positive effects relative to individual choice and sense of personal power. The "increased-responsibility" group reported they felt happier and more active than the residents in the comparison group. These residents were rated for alertness by the interviewer and again the "increased-responsibility" group exhibited higher alertness. Combined, these differences in ratings were statistically validating. The nurses' ratings exceeded the other measurements, showing an even greater difference over the previous measurements, all verifying that greater responsibility promoted better overall health. Conversely, the comparison group was seen to decline in general. Of the reduced-responsibility group, only one subject had measurably improved: 93% of the increased-responsibility group improved.

The "increased-responsibility" group began visiting others more and more, and engaged in conversations for considerably longer periods of time, engaging less in passive activities like watching the staff. Movie attendance was found to go up significantly in the "increased responsibility" group, and ten fourth-floor residents participated in the jellybean contest guessing (versus only one from the second floor). Follow-up studies indicated that the "increased-responsibility" group continued to be in better condition than the other residents. Doctors reported that the "increased responsibility" group showed an increase in overall health. By contrast, a slight decline was evidenced in the other residents.

Langer and Rodin indicated that this study, in addition to other earlier experiments, demonstrated that people who have had their control taken away, and their decision-making powers removed experience a decrease in overall levels of well being. These same individuals, given a greater sense of personal responsibility, changed their attitudes and their behaviors. Their lives were visibly affected, producing more pro-social behaviors and greater health.

A study of individuals living with spinal cord injuries found that they measured the satisfaction in their living conditions by the amount of control and choice they perceived they had, not the level of care they were given or even the severity of their disabilities.[4]

Results of Powerless in Prison

The conclusions of all these studies surely have relevance human experience in other settings, and especially for those who are forced to live in an institutional setting. Human beings have an intrinsic need to exercise personal responsibility, which allows them to perceive that they have personal choice. Control and perceptions of self-power are relevant to happiness, sociability and health.

Today, the very human need for personal control and some sense of autonomy can best be seen in what manifests when it does not exist. In WCCW, women struggle to find a method by which to effect change, in their personal endeavor to establish some degree of control in their lives. Those without the interpersonal skills needed to adapt to a very unnatural environment will start to engage in self-mutilating acts or suicide attempts, or develop eating disorders,

---

4. Boschen, 1996

bulimia, and obesity. These are prevalent, and addicting in nature, as they serve the goal of making an act of autonomy. That a woman, unlike a man, will inflict self-injury, internalizing the expression of psychic angst through her own personal sacrifice, deserves reflection. Women who act out violently toward others are exceptional.

Why do some women manage to function inside the limits and handle the stresses of institutional living while many do not? Women are obviously not all equal in emotional strength when they enter prison. Histories of severe chaos and dysfunction may predispose some woman to self-injurious behaviors. Such coping methods may continue for years.

Another study of the elderly confined in nursing homes has revealed that self-destructive acts are not uncommon (although outright suicide is rare).[5] Similar to the WCCW population's behaviors, the elderly in nursing homes purposely choose to not eat, and may refuse to take critical medications, even when the refusal is potentially fatal. In their findings, Conwell, Pearson, and Derenzo reason that such dangerous act by residents could be extreme cries for help, in response to feelings of powerlessness over their environment. These actions are the only opportunity available to them to exercise control over their environment.

These exact behaviors are seen among the population in WCCW also. One woman, a mother who constantly grieves the separation and lack of contact with her children, tried to commit suicide by jumping head first off a fifteen-foot upper level. She failed, and her next serious attempt was to burn herself alive. She poured nail polish on her upper torso and lit herself on fire. She was hospitalized for severe burns and required skin grafts.

Another mother was losing custody of her children and couldn't endure the emotional anguish; she swallowed cleaning detergent, Tylenol, and medications. When the extreme pain began, she notified staff; they, instead of calling for medical intervention, placed her in administrative segregation (the "Hole"), where she died hours later. That was in the early 1980s.

Another mother hanged herself, and died. These are not the only cases of suicide in WCCW's short history (30 years), but they serve to illustrate the intolerable desperation that can overtake these women. Unlike the nursing homes patients, they did have a release date. And, of course, they had been convicted of a crime. However, there is some question as to how much responsibility the system has in such incidents; further on, this study will cite some of the elements that put these women in prison.

---

5. Conwell, Pearson, and Derenzo, 1996.

In TEC: An Extreme Environment

This relates directly to the conditions I found in TEC, where I initiated several pro-active programs in 1999 in response to the disturbing rumors going around. Through the prison grapevine, information is passed via word of mouth. Gossip about the personal behaviors of other women and staff, including their presumed economic status and living habits, is part of this inner circle of information exchange; some is malicious and inaccurate, but it is informative in its own way. Inmate to staff, staff to volunteer, staff to inmate: the lines occasionally blur.

I received information about restrictions that were being imposed on these "mentally ill" women under the rationale of "security," for "their own safety and progress." Restrictions in the TEC living environment were applied without compensatory helpful stimulations. These women were really in an isolation ward: no books, no art, no positive group interaction — all of which combined to create a condition prisoners refer to as "psychological terrorism."

Alarmed by these reports, I started to do some reading. Among the most telling materials I found was the research by M. R. Rosenzweig, who studied the effect of an impoverished environment versus an enriched environment on brain growth and chemistry in rats. Later, in response to criticisms that "differential handling" may have skewed the results, Rosenzweig and his colleagues repeated the work, this time using wild deer mice instead of laboratory rats, testing the effects of a natural outdoor environment versus enriched laboratory cages. The results were clear. The greater access the mice had to mixed stimuli, the more their brain synapses grew (by as much as 50%).

During examination by autopsy and brain dissection, weight and size measurements were taken and the electron microscope was used to detect levels of cell growth and neurotransmitter activity. The original tests with laboratory rats showed larger neurons; a higher ratio of RNA to DNA (brain chemicals for cell growth); higher ratio of weight of cortex to the rest of the brain; and higher levels of acetylcholinesterase, an enzyme which allows for faster and more efficient transmission of impulses among brain cells — all a by-product response to the enriched environment. Rosenzweig's later studies with wild deer mice in a natural environment versus an enriched laboratory environment found that the natural environment surpassed the enriched laboratory environment, providing a greater brain-stimulating situation.

All this suggested to me something that might be happening in the impoverished TEC environment. Granted, the theory that "more experience equals bigger brain" is based on mice and rats, but the potential applications in human mental health were intriguing and worthy of extrapolation.

My own quest for answers as to why the TEC women fared so poorly provoked me to ask some questions about myself, to discover the answers to my own psychological riddle: Why did I become who I became, and how did I change my own life script?

As my self-discovery unfolded, I was able to share some of the information I was uncovering with other women here; likewise, they offered their insights in support groups, seminars, workshops, tutoring, and writing. Self-growth and discovery is an ongoing education for me. That was both incentive and reward for involving myself in the situation in TEC. Following the precedents I had set by creating new programs and managing workshops and seminars for the general population, I decided to see what could be done to provide support services to the women in the prison's mental ward unit.

A Step in the Right Direction

My own experience with abuse and the responses to the abuse I experienced gave me deep empathy for these women, who were still suffering so deeply. To assist them by providing opportunities in which they could make choices and receive positive information through books, while sharing as they desired, seemed a reasonable objective. My early efforts in this direction had minimal impact, but with persistence and patience, gains were made.

The TEC Betterment Program began, and my requests for help from volunteers to assist in my work were beginning to get approved. My focus expanded. As my work led me deeper into the women's personal stories and their diagnosed "personality disorders-label identities," I found I was being asked to help write letters, explain paperwork, and interpret the materials from which these labels were garnered. This, I explained, I could not do, not only because of the readily apparent ethical issues, but because I hadn't the specialized knowledge. My work was to assist in basic letter-writing to attorneys, staff and family members, not serve as a paralegal or therapist. However, the women's stories were disturbing, riveting, and highly charged with abuse histories. I began experiencing something like a transfer of their despairs.

I was finding it more and more difficult to enter the unit when certain staff members were on duty. The hostility these particular employees emanated provoked flashbacks of my own past abuse. I could sense that my work and the work of my team of volunteers was rocking the apple cart; a power struggle was going on, and evolved into a covert war waged by these officers. Their weapons included excessive pat searches of everyone involved in the program, incident reports, canceling of programs, interference with participants, and confiscation of pre-approved items (glue sticks, magic markers and so on).

As volunteers would check in with me for a debrief, on an as-needed basis, some would come with tears in their eyes and repeat stories of the harassment that particular staff directed not only at the TEC inmates but at the Betterment volunteers as well. All I could do at the time was to take notes of the reported incident and calm the volunteer down, reassuring them that this would be addressed with the unit supervisor. It was upsetting for me to assist them in processing out the experience when I knew these traumas were part and parcel of the demands made on any volunteer with the fortitude to even contemplate work in the most oppressive quarters of the institution. Due to this harassment, the volunteer dropout rate increased — understandably so.

Control issues within institutional settings are notorious for their excess, as Rodin and Langer report. They can also have debilitating ramifications for the residents involved. Within the U.S. Department of Justice, the Center on Crime, Communities and Culture has reported that the rates of mental illness in prison populations are at least double the rate among civilians of the general population. Prior to incarceration, 16% of inmates were either in a mental institution or had an overnight stay in one. Mentally ill offenders also serve on average 15 months longer in prison than other inmates, because their symptoms of delusions and paranoia or hallucinations make them disciplinary problems.

There are 8 times as many mentally ill people in prisons as there are in state hospitals. That is frightening. Legislative parsimony has pushed women out of mental hospitals and into prison; that is an appalling disgrace in a $7 trillion economy. Nearly 1 out of 5 violent offenders in prison or on probation is mentally ill. During incarceration, these mentally ill inmates are more likely to get into fights and 33% of the men and 48% women were victims of physical abuse and or sexual abuse prior to their incarceration. Some WCCW staff report that local statistics regarding female offenders in general suggest the rate of prior historical physical and or sexual abuse is as high as 80%.

Clinical psychologist Dorothy Lewis and Yale neurologist John Pincus conducted numerous state of the art tests on violent juvenile offenders and discovered remarkable abnormalities in the CAT scan, MRT, and EEGs of their subjects. (These tests measure electrical patterns and other conditions in the brain.) Lewis asserts that child abuse impairs the development of the cortex. When the frontal lobe (the part of the cortex behind the forehead) is damaged by severe head injuries from batterings (or car accidents), ongoing abuses will result in impulsivity, impaired judgment and faulty processing of vital data needed to determine appropriate responses and behaviors with the environment.

Our brains are so delicate and sensitive to trauma that even something as simple as shocking news can have lasting affects. The brain has a stress response system which, when activated by trauma, triggers a chain of neurological events Adrenal glands emit a hormone called cortisol. When trauma is unrelenting, the levels of cortisol within the brain become so excessive that it literally begins eating away the cortex. I think of this phenomenon as similar to a stomach which develops ulcers, which in turn aggravate the esophagus, eroding the internal tissues. Acids which are helpful when our bodies are in homeostasis can become corrosive when over stimulated or are present in excess, and damage our internal parts.

Cortisol in itself is part of our body's way of alerting and coping with potential adversarial situations, a registering of being out of homeostasis. Emergency reactions mediated by the autonomic nervous system, primarily the reticular activating systems of the brain stem, the hypothalamus and pituitary gland (the HPA axis), alters the internal neurochemistry that regulates our thinking and behaviors. Changes in cerebral blood flow and the turnover of central transmitters such as norepinephrine noradrenalin), dopamine, serotonin and acetycholine are mostly temporary; however, when trauma is unrelenting or extreme, particularly when it takes place before a person is fully grown, microstructural internal changes can occur which permanently affect neurochemistry.

WCCW's TEC houses the women who are diagnosed with mental illness or developmental handicaps. Given the oral histories these women shared with me while I visited them in TEC, I believe that reactions to trauma are a significant part of the story. For them to attain any degree of success in independent functioning, they need specialized resources and assistance. The programs I began sought to open windows of exploration in these directions.

The results of these efforts were dramatic. Self-injuries inside the unit went down; in fact, eventually the rate was less than in the general population at WCCW. It had been double. I credit the success in rehabilitation to more than these programs; there has to be empathy and patience from the hands-on facilitators, or the program just doesn't work. With a team of staff members that shared the same vision I had, the Superintendent and several sergeants and others, and the women volunteers (also inmates), all acting courageously, broke new ground together. Understanding the legal, political and social risks, we forged ahead regardless. I have chosen to omit the names of DOC personnel, since they still could endure a backlash of retribution from unappreciative colleagues within this sclerotic bureaucracy. Mutual compassion rewrote the history of the prison, transforming it from what it was to what it could be.

Together, we made a difference in enriching the lives of not just the TEC inmates, these fragile and forgotten women, but ourselves as well.

Unfortunately, Department of Corrections staff are frequently relocated and, over time, so were the members of the team I worked with. With the new staff replacements and personal changes in my own life, I had to retire from my own work at TEC to write this report.

8. The Effects of Abuse

Post-Traumatic Stress Disorder

I have spoken with hundreds of women prisoners who related to me their psychological symptomology in the quest to unburden themselves of the fear they were "crazy." They sought my reassurance and support. I learned that the vast majority of these women were victims of a history of early and repeated abuse. Often, they were labeled by the courts as a serious threat to the community, antisocial, dangerous, etc.

A clear pattern of stereotyping by prosecutors statewide, routinely categorizing these women without regard to circumstance, created reports that are simply cliche. "Reprobate," "incorrigible," and "unworthy" were stigmas that then lifted themselves off the paperwork and followed the women. It is no coincidence, I think, that histories of being abused are coupled with histories of subsequent substance abuse and co-dependent behaviors.

Self-inflicted injuries are not unusual with this population. Institutional reports of such behaviors are often classified as "manipulative": calls for attention; attempts to elicit sympathy. These simplistic views lack real any true sense of these coping mechanisms. Profoundly significant losses in identity can be suffered by victims of abuse, and these losses continue to be felt after the events have ended. Post-Traumatic Stress Disorder (Complex PTSD) in women can reach an extreme.

Only within the last six years has CPTSD been recognized. Judith Herman's work, *Trauma and Recovery*, is still being digested among academics; institutional applications in real terms are yet to be realized. Despite the knowledge that the vast majority of women who are incarcerated and who are victims of abuse need specialized care, the system has not yet allocated funds for such treatment.

Trauma Re-Enactment Syndrome, by Dusty Miller, is an example of a women-oriented study of some relevance here (one of the few that I could find). If applied to criminal behavior in women, Miller's therapeutic models could assist in curbing female recidivism. Therapeutic intervention to prevent recidivism will only work if it is implemented correctly, and only if that therapeutic model addresses the real needs of its clients. Standard male treatments may work for men yet not work for women. Understanding the female first, and then using a gender-specific remedy, has to begin if we desire to treat women fairly and equally under the law.

Today, WCCW women continue to self-medicate, substance abuse and/or self-injure, despite attempts at intervention. Later, these women will return to the dysfunctional relationships that led them to WCCW. Behaviors repeat until something new and powerful offers convincing opportunities to change. Punishment will not stop crime. As a tragic consequence of this, children are left behind. Alone and vulnerable, they are shuffled through a system of foster-care services that remain overtaxed and terribly flawed, causing a new trauma to these children.

Examples of CPTSD are women who use substance abuse to cope with flashbacks, panic attacks, dissociative states, and insomnia. Drugs or alcohol can be forms of self-medicating or numbing.[6] Eating disorders, self-injury — whatever can block the feelings and thoughts that are too painful and frightening to face. Triggers that provoke flashbacks and trauma-recalls stimulate brain processes. These processes are the switches that turn on and off glandular activity, which produces biochemical reactions that speed up the heart rate, altering the brains pathways and receptor cite communications.[7]

We might think of CPTSD as a malfunction of an otherwise benign survival mechanism. Think of being in a car accident: your body is pinned inside, crushed between the steering wheel and seat. Now, someone who is oblivious to your pain and crisis approaches you, asking you to help solve an algebra equation he's working on. Could you do it? Would you be inclined to try? Of course not.

---

6. Herman, J.
7. Niehoff, D.

Your body is so pumped with chemical responses, and your level of alarm and pain would prevent you from being focused on anything but your situation and how to get free from the car. These internal reactions are all a survival response enacted in neuro-transmitter language.

Mothers who experience a burst of phenomenal strength and lift cars ten times their own weight to save their child are another example of the power of this great neuro-transmitter capability. For victims with CPTSD, this chemical language is triggered to go on and off without the car wreck, without the child under the tire.

The same way your brain works in the car wreck example is how many women with abuse histories are functioning on a daily basis. Imagine, suddenly you are instantly transported out from behind that driving wheel, suddenly no longer pinned; you are zapped back to your work office and your boss is telling you to do this paperwork now. — Can you do it? Do you instantly shrug off the terror and fear and emotional surges? Or do you need a pill to relax you, maybe two or three pills, to push aside the terror and get back on track? But that is only the beginning of the problem for those who suffer from CPTSD. If it ended there, the woman would only be severely handicapped in ordinary life.

Commonsense would lead most people to accept the analogy I presented above, but commonsense tends to reject the idea that those who are victimized can so easily and involuntarily become victimizers. The women I dealt with had gone beyond to the point of committing criminal acts.

To understand how a victim becomes a perpetrator or "acts out" inappropriately, we need to look at the popular social trends that define a female victim. When the female experiences trauma through victimization, is she supported or protected from further violation? Does the law enforcement as funded by the public dollar look to her recovery and rehabilitation?

Mostly, we know the answer is No, to each of these questions. When the victim finds herself alone, with an injured self-concept on top of other more obvious injuries, and the stigma of being a victim, and when she is unable to stop further abuse or fails to "just get over it," the victim responds by an adaptation response: dysfunctional coping methods and often patterns of behavior that insure her likelihood of re-victimization.

These coping methods are all related, in that they are distortions of something healthy into behavior that is hurtful: substance abuse, dysfunctional relationships, eating disorders, and self-harming. Crime is a likely outcome for two reasons. First, a person who is systematically violated with impunity comes to doubt the rightness of the conventional moral order and seeks to accommodate the violator. This now has a name: the Stockholm Syndrome. Second, when this goes on for a long time, the belief in the underlying rightness and goodness of the moral order that is the foundation of law gives way to an overwhelming determination to survive at whatever cost to others. A part of the victim's mind still knows this act is wrong, but in such a wrongful world, the price of rightness is simply too high. Here, we come to crime, then incarceration, and recidivism if the pattern is left to continue without intervention.

Once introduced into the present system of Corrections, the victim's identity is now sealed, as is her fate and the fate of her family. No longer the "victim"; she is the "offender," and any revelation of her own history of abuse is used against her as "just her excuse" to rationalize her crime. She is labeled as manipulative, anti-social, and immature for failing to take responsibility. Little if any help is offered to her except for a few group sessions, which are limited in time and membership. Her defense mechanisms are methods she uses to cope with stressors; they are automatic psychological processes that keep anxiety at bay. Unfortunately, they create a vicious cycle that self-perpetuates. The routine becomes habitual and very difficult to break.

Attendance at a group session once a week for an hour, over a brief 12 weeks (facilitated by one social worker whose attention is divided by 10 to 15 women needing help) does not bode well for success. The inmate's participation is all too often inhibited by fear of peer ridicule if she exposes all of her self-abuse, and the "disease to please" curtails her disclosure to relatively harmless matters. With low self-esteem, she will tend to hide further into her coping methods, some times picking up a new habit in the process.

Institutional staff members are trained to beware of the women, as they can become victims of their manipulations. Staff are briefed about the high level of anti-social personalities that fill the prison and this means the inmates are not to be trusted. This, in turn, leads to staff being especially hardened, defensive, and critically opposed to the inmates. No longer are these women with histories of abuse, victimized and suffering the tremendous despairs of their loss of children and home and freedom; they have become an enemy. They are now often viewed as the criminal: cold, lacking conscience and moral values, plotting to exploit all in their path, capable of any treachery and cruelty, incapable of remorse, growth, and rehabilitation. The woman has lost her human status and is a potentially lethal threat.

This is not as gross an exaggeration as we would like to assume. Rather, the tendency to think in the elementary method of black and white is what keeps society placing these women in a male environment. The dysfunctional behaviors of the women flourish behind the walls. The staff are accustomed to self-mutilation and suicide attempts, which they routinely presume are either crazy or manipulative acts. They see nothing in the women who do this beyond the event itself. These self-harming acts are easier to detect than the more insidious ones that exist in co-dependent abusive relationships and eating disorders.

Stressors trigger coping behaviors. There exists a correlation to abuse and dysfunctional behaviors beyond substance abuse and criminal expression. Prior abuse histories in the women polled in this study are extraordinarily high. We have yet to create a complete definition of dysfunctional response behaviors in victimized women, and therefore we have yet to measure these behaviors with accuracy; but when we do, keys to the female felon's rehabilitation can assist in designing successful programs for these women.

The "non-incarcerated" female victim maybe socially penalized for her self-harming and dysfunctional characteristics too, although these are, if understood, only victim responses to unresolved traumas. For the incarcerated female who does the same kind of thing, there is a methodology in Corrections which only tends to further isolate and estrange her from her society, perpetuating her victimization.

I believe government policy is profoundly wrong and injurious to its citizens when a society maintains social order by employing a methodology that ignores the plight of its victims. Today's victims may prove tomorrow's offenders, and that fact is statistically established by the WCCW findings on histories of inmates' prior abuse. Where a woman crosses the line between acceptable "acting-out" and non-acceptable actions is subjective and moral only if one excludes her victimization.

Today, we as a society separate mothers from their children — and we call this intervention. The gross cost in tax dollars to intervene in this way is far more than the cost would be if we provided family education and mediation that seeks to build and educate, heal and inform, rather than foster care, court costs, prisons, and so forth.

Presently, women are measured by male standards and empirical findings based on male-identified research that, like our medical data, is applied as non-gender-specific truth. Male crimes, male aggression, male institutional behavior, male mental health studies, male-designed prisons, male clothing, male social-ization studies, and research conducted on men are used across the board, while their suitability remains virtually unexamined. I argue that women are different from men in how we express our aggression and deal with our victimization. Today, there are researchers who share this viewpoint.[8]

Crimes committed by women should be addressed in a separate court. What we are doing now is perpetuating misogyny and institutionalizing it by

---

8. see Caplen, P. 1995

meting out the correctional standards we as a society now promote. Non-gender distinction in correctional methodology is non-sense.

I assert this from the vantage point of a first-hand experienced participant. Twenty years of conversations with literally thousands of women felons, coupled with first hand observation of their perspectives, behaviors and attitudes, have forged this viewpoint. I have worked in numerous capacities within the prison: I've witnessed the inter-generational legacy of so-called "female criminality" perpetuated from grandmother, to mother, to daughter, to sister, with a regularity that is frightening. Patterns of dysfunction are the real "criminality."

Relevant to this are the spoken and unspoken messages the women communicate to each other about who they are and what they can't and can't do in the world around them. By choices made and actions not taken, these silent patterns and behaviors speak volumes in the construction of a girl's identity and perception of the world around her.

Each subsequent generation inherits this inappropriate belief system, despite the self-destructive and painful attitudes this faulty self-concept guarantees. These women are socially pressed into this pattern of subjugation and defeat, regardless of their best efforts.[9]

I argue against the platitudes offered by those very few who "pull themselves up by their own boot straps." They claim that if one person can survive and make it out of an underdog position, so can everyone else. Reality demonstrates otherwise. It is this very reasoning which maintains the status quo of victimization in our society, by reducing trauma to an issue of personal choice "to get over it, or not."

The assumption that choice exists for most of these women is erroneous, at least as choice is ordinarily conceived. Consider the individuals who, during World War II, gave up their loyalty to their minority communities and went to work in the concentration camps, to save their own lives. Search the pages of our peoples' histories, our tales of war and what our non-criminal predecessors did when faced with the tragedies and traumas of victimization and survival.[10] We learn by experience, and in the view of these victims, escape does not register as an option.

New scientific studies with brain imaging and radioactive tracers present a new scientific confirmation of the physical effects of trauma. Monitoring neuronal response mechanisms within the power control centers of the brain, trauma's history is illustrated in structural damages and malfunctions in victims

---

9. Estes 1970)
10. Grossman 1995)

surviving extreme trauma; they cripple the brain, preventing it from accessing higher levels of reasoning that modify and control our responses to external stimuli, our behaviors. Can these damages be worked with or healed, so that crime does not reoccur? Yes, they can, with help, training, opportunities and education. Some pioneering programs are already showing stirring examples of success.[11]

Otherwise, social reinforcements keep these women dispossessed from entering functional roles in society. Where their victimization begins and ends may well be dictated prior to birth. For, once victimization begins, and it usually begins very early, it has no end for most victims, unless intervention and opportunities are brought forth.

Those lucky few who survive chronic abuse and come out seemingly unscathed are not just lucky, they possess inner tools and opportunities. These same inner tools and opportunities need to be created for the other women in prison. Not only is it possible to do, but it can be done with shifts in policy and creative brainstorming. As Heraclitus said: "Character is fate." And so it will continue to be — until we learn that character has a huge social component. What abuse (which is certainly social) has done, an understanding alteration of actual circumstances and appropriate changes in life can undo. The beginning is simply the recognition that what has made one "criminal" or "crazy" may have been victimization through abuse.

Recognizing Abuse: The Victim's Awareness Manual

Case Management is the system used by the Department of Corrections to address the offenders' identified needs. It entails required participation in various classes. The top of this list is the Victim Awareness course, which all inmates must attend prior to their release. The course is built around a workbook, in which assignments are given. A female inmate defines abuse and neglect by the particulars she is taught; for most of them, the term never existed prior to their coming to prison.

To introduce the class participants to this new view of "abuse," here is an annotated excerpt from the handbook.

---

11. Dr. Corinne Gerwe tells the stories of individual patients and gives a general description of her rehabilitation program for the Georgia State Corrections system in *The Orchestration of Joy and Suffering, Understanding Chronic Addiction* (Algora Publishing: 2001). Her work, based on an understanding of the effects of trauma in early childhood, is so successful that the National Peace Foundation has asked her to create a program in Russia.

Profile of Neglect

This section provides an interesting look at not only at a person's pre-incarceration history (identifying problematic areas many of the inmates are already familiar with), but also happens to serve as a reminder of their current situation and the environment in prison. The top section highlights various aspects that define neglect by parents. Ironically, many or all of the characteristics can be pinned on Prison in its role as ward or guardian for the incarcerated person.

[The book notes that neglectful parents:]

1. "Exhibit behaviors of despair and defeat." This certainly exemplifies how the mother feels in prison. The inmate mother sees her societal parental figure (the prison) in its response to her. Prison as an expression of society is an ever-present fact, the inmate mother sees. Society has given up on her, and condones having her children taken from her; after all, she is "bad."

2. "Do not have defined family role responsibilities." The inmate no longer a mother; she is an "offender." The prison attempts to provide an extended parental role by way of housing and rule maintenance, yet also is the accuser and prosecutor in her life, continuously defining her as "offender."

3. "Seem indifferent to the problems and behaviors of their children." On one hand, the inmate mother loves and worries over her children's plight. She will go to staff for phone calls or visits, seeking help to reach out to her children which she is told, in her classes, is a good thing. The reality is that staff cannot provide scan calls and cannot intervene with visitation problems, nor spare the time to address the mother's grieving. D.O.C. budgetary restrictions and mandated neutrality require that staff "don't give the female offender something that the men don't get." All this works to foreclose her contact with her children.

4. "Do not work, talk, or play with each other." Here, the inmate mother is in a bind. Clearly she cannot have opportunities to do this unless she has a family member outside who is willing to bring the child to the prison programs. This is costly and requires proof of guardianship or custody rights; otherwise, the caregiver for the inmate's child cannot bring the child in. Often, the cost, in terms of gas or other transportation expense, time, emotional strain and so forth make it impossible.

5. "Live without the regard to adult friendship networks." The networks for many of these mothers are dysfunctional and crime-related. The inmate has not been able to fit into a functional network of friendship relationships; or, those that were once possible, now reject her for her "offender" stigma.

6. "Expend much time and energy meeting crises." Crises are part of survival. Histories of abuse are dictated by survival and crisis. Prison produces

many more, by way of custody battles with the state, relocation, stigma upon release.

7. "Expend little energy planning for ordinary, recurring family needs." Once in prison, a visit is a crisis, as it is nearly impossible for the mothers to provide the least help for her children's obvious needs.

8. "Leave young children alone for long periods of time." Jail, then prison, make abandonment a given. The children respond as defined in the continuing profile of neglect.

9. "Home." The realm of despair that is prison is now the mother's home. Prison offers little refuge or privacy for the adult with a visiting child, as most visits are restricted to the visiting room, an awkwardly artificial environment. Prison has frequent emergencies. Prison does not offer the routine of commonly shared meals or chores or socializing for a mother and her children except for those few involved in the trailer visit family program. Prison evokes gloom and apathy, especially for mothers as they express their tendency to obsess over their children. Even for visitors, prison by its very structure and the circumstances involved, creates an unwelcoming atmosphere.

Countless women have refused to cooperate with police officials upon their arrest, so it's easy to label them incorrigible and desirous of committing offenses. After all, why aren't they telling the detective that the man ordered them to do it.

As the Victim's Awareness Manual says, "She will be punished," and unfortunately, as a woman, the stakes are raised. Nothing silences a victim like pre-conditioning begun in childhood. Who are these silenced women? They are the children this book defines, [now] grown-up. The cycle now reached a full fruition. Abused child, abused adolescent, abused woman, and incarcerated mother.[12]

"No one will believe her." The list goes on and on. Most, if not all, women of this era will never know the true power that a male experiences. The societal processing which has been transmitted inter-generationally by our culture is such that unless you are a woman you cannot feel its effects.

The female victim is perhaps alone in her near complete apprehension of this phenomenon (her dead victim sisters having felt it to the maximum). Until we can acknowledge their experience and its enduring ramifications, the rising rate of mothers in prison, and their subsequent failure to "just *get over* it," will not cease.

The Correctional Education Association's declaration eloquently warns against "window dressing" and its failure to meet the aspirations of the educator.

---

12. page 57 in the Victim's Awareness Manual

The reforming of the female "offender" will come about in equal measure to society's reforming of its view and the strategies women's prisons implement.

The solutions in part are already demonstrated in the ideas of the "peer-educator" and "inmate-facilitator." These are our greatest untapped resources. The inmates themselves can and must be viewed as potentially valuable allies for our communities. Those who wish to play this role must be integrated into our current Department of Corrections agendas and we must supply opportunities for their training and later implementation into the educational system. The Victim Awareness Program Manual is an excellent tool, which should be used beyond the classroom setting and put into the prison dayrooms. Educators within the C.E.A. need to be given a forum in which their knowledge can be used to create such programs.

Women are empowered by being validated — validated as human beings who can change, can help others, can provide services for others in the prison itself. But prison as it now operates will never provide the solution to stop crime. It is a male solution for a male-created environment of crime.

Women, as this study has discovered, have emotional needs and backgrounds unlike those of men. There are, indeed, gender distinctions, although they have been submerged as the wave of the Equal Rights Amendment has flooded our legislative forum. Now is the time to delve deeper into the needs of our women, starting with those living through the backlash of political change.

Voices of the Innocent

I don't think the public or the system want to believe that a lot of us women are actually innocent of a crime. If they cared or wanted the truth, they'd listen. No one wants to listen, or maybe they like knowing we are here. I can't tell staff that I'm innocent, because the mental health people will write terrible things about me. I must be a liar, or trying to manipulate; it's a real horror. Before this happened to me, I never believed innocent people were tried for crimes. I thought: well, for the detectives and the attorney general's office to prosecute someone, they must have some real evidence against the accused, not some story that they just conjure up so they can get a damn promotion or because it's election year and a conviction will look good on their record. Then I had my day in court, and facts were distorted, outright lies were said and believed, so I was found guilty before I ever went to trial. Guilty of lies of what never happened.

When I got here, I felt so alone — until I heard a few others tell their stories and it hit me, then — Oh God, this has happened to more women than me.

Now, after so many years, I've just come to accept that, yeah, a lot of us are absolutely without responsibility for whatever came down. Or facts were twisted. I can't estimate how many here are here for things they didn't do; I can think of about twenty of us, but there are more. We're scared to speak out, though, because no one believes us; then we're punished by the system for saying we are innocent.

I don't believe in justice, there just isn't any — you're about as likely to win a lottery. Once someone alleges something about you, you're guilty. In fact, if I accused someone of something, staff or volunteer, I could set up their worst nightmare. People out there in the free world just haven't a clue. One day they'll be the one walking in my shoes and they'll think, "shit, why didn't I ever do anything to help change the system?

I pleaded guilty to a crime I didn't commit, to save my family from shame and pain. I could've jumped bail and let my family lose their home that they put up for eight months of my freedom, just to come here and do this time. I'm here now, and I will get out, and live to tell about my hardships and nightmares that I go through here now and everyday of this eleven year sentence I'm doing.

Marlene

9. TEC and the Beginnings of Betterment

As the prison's Mental Health unit, observation and evaluation are two principle functions provided. The unit is divided into two small wings: the Residential, in which the women at less severe risk are held, and the Acute side for those requiring 15-minute checks. The Residential inmates, having successfully transitioned out of the Acute side, are supposed to obtain greater levels of freedom as they graduate through phases of stability and prove their competency to assume responsibility for themselves. The phased-in privileges begin with outside yard time and the option to use the main institution library. Meals are also taken in the main institution, under escort. The women are seated at a designated table. The real perk is that this provides them with one more opportunity to smoke, on the way to and from the meal. Those women who suffer from anxiety attacks, agoraphobia, delusions and related problems have the option of having a tray delivered to the unit.

Canteen and recreational services are extremely limited, and although they may wear the same gray sweatsuits as other inmates when they are granted the privilege of going to the dining hall, theirs are branded in big black letters, "TEC," unmistakably distinguishing them from the general population. Similar to the other units, the dayrooms have large round metal tables with small round seats, all steel, and cold. There are televisions, but only one per wing. Unlike the rest of the prison's dayrooms, the rules in TEC do not permit personal televisions — only radios, if one has attained the phase level requirement.

Video cameras are monitored from inside the staff observation post. Correctional officers rarely remain inside the living areas, beyond the occasions when their keys are needed to open doors. There are group meetings within the Unit on a bi-weekly basis, facilitated by a counselor or psychologist (when one is available).

The Acute wing has single-cell occupancy only. There are no activities beyond the use of crayons and children's coloring books. Occasionally, a woman may be seen watching television during the approved hours. The wing is disturbing to most people who enter on tour or for brief visits; the predominant impression is the sound of women crying and a series of faces exuding depression and fear, all crammed in tiny concrete quarters and a colorless environment. It can be overwhelming.

The unit is designed to reduce external stimuli. The primitive psychological understanding of those who make policy for TEC subscribes to the belief that too much stimulation may trigger their underlying disorders. Meanwhile, one has no idea at all of what is going on in the minds of these women. What has been overlooked is that the environment provides highly oppressive and depressing stimuli in itself by offering only the visual misery of the others, their audible voices sobbing in despair; all without distractions.

The screening process that places women in this unit uses the diagnostic specifications identified in their inmate profile. Every category of disorder is housed in TEC: Schizophrenia, Schizophreniform, Borderline Personality Disorder, Bipolar I and II, Munchausen Syndrome and Munchausen by proxy, Alzheimer's disease, severe cases of diabetes, Post Traumatic Stress Disorder with severe symptomology, Dissociative Disorder, various categories of depression, eating disorders, developmental disabilities (mental retardation), and other diagnoses of personality or behavioral problems.

Prior to my work in TEC, I skimmed the DSM-III Diagnostic Statistical Manual, the tool used by psychiatrists and psychologists to determine the "proper" clinical label assigned to the subject's symptoms. To select the label-identity, the clinician must screen the subject's complex of symptoms. This determination relies on the previous empirical data and published theoretical findings, conducted for the most part by male researchers studying male subjects; these findings were combined to create the DSM reference handbook. A secondary point must also be understood in the process of the clinician's determination. In forming a diagnosis, a clinician must rely on subjective reasoning. Subjective, here, means characteristic of or belonging to reality as *perceived* rather than as independent objective reality. Often, this subjectivity means relating to experience or knowledge as conditioned by personal mental characteristics or states arising from conditions within the brain or sense organs and not directly caused by external stimuli. Sometimes it arises out of, or is identified by, means of one's perception of one's own states and processes and is not observable by an examiner (according to Merriam-Webster's Medical Dictionary, 1999.) As disconcerting as it may be to the person making it or the person accepting it, the judgment call in forming a label-identity is not as precise a science as 1+1=2. Yet with all this opportunity for error, the labels attached to the women in prison are treated held to be unquestionable. As I read the diagnoses of the women I encountered and tried to fit the technical terms to the way they actually live, I became increasingly disenchanted with those words that seemed to say so much about a person but take absolutely no account of her life history.

I found more studies that suggested the harm that is done by living in a stimulus-deprived environment. Some research found that enriched experiences may increase the secretion of certain neurotransmitter chemicals which enhance learning.[13] Schore, using Rosenzweig's ideas of environmental factors during the critical growth period (birth to 2 years of age), found that negative environments produced lasting heightened susceptibility to various psychological disorders later in life.[14] Langer and Rodin's studies show the behavior aspect of this theory. I began to think that negative environments happening to persons later in life might have effects of their own. And here were these women, so casually diagnosed as having intractable mental problems, when their behaviors might be being exacerbated rather than ameliorated by the environment they were forced to endure.

For example, in a prison setting, the differences between a TEC ward and a general population environment are obvious, the former being deprived, dull and depressing and the latter, though meager, relatively enriched and natural. While inside TEC, inmates wear white or orange uniforms. The General Population mostly wears civilian clothing. TEC is an isolation or restricted unit — real confinement. The General Population has some access to school, a library, gym, and so on.

Due to the nature of TEC operations, all possible items that could be a potential threat are removed from the inmates. If such precautionary measures were enforced in a reasonable manner, the principle would serve the unit's needs effectively; however, characteristically, institutional implementation of what is logically sound is overcompensated in this area.

And while it makes sense that TEC should have some degree of censorship of literary content, it seems to be an overstretch when novels, books, magazines

---

13. Bennett, E. L., 1976 and Woody, C., 1986.
14. Schore, A., 1996.

are so restricted as this: no hard bound, no stapled magazines, no content that is "stimulating" in any way, as it may provoke an outburst. While this may sound appropriate, on the surface, in practice this policy has been used to turn away *all* literature except for a few religious tracts and romance novels.

For those living under such restrictions, excessive loss of stimuli can exacerbate the very behaviors and the psychological instability the unit was intended to correct or control. That was my hunch, confirmed by the scientific findings; and the success of our work in not only bringing the women out of their apathy but in drastically reducing the incidence of disruptive behavior now proves that we were right.

Before we could make more than the smallest changes in the dreary hell that was TEC, the law intervened to give things a push. A class action lawsuit was filed on behalf of the women of TEC by Columbia Legal Services, after letters were written and complaints lodged about these and other serious issues. Once the courts became involved, following the death of some of those who were mentally, emotionally and/or physically injured through gross neglect and abuse, a team of inspectors began examining the allegations. Their findings and the statements by the staff who headed these areas of concern led the court to order redress and remedy by the state. The proverbial buck never quite found a stopping place, but there was finally at least some humane concern and attention to the situation by the more enlightened part of the system and a good deal of anxiety on the part of even the most callous and unenlightened. An impenetrable wall had been breached; it was uncertain what might pass through that opening.

It was a time when there was genuinely a belief that something should be done. Bureaucracies, though, are much better at doing more of the same old thing than coming up with an appropriate response when their very method of operation has been found at fault. I made up my mind to float a proposal. In response to the perceived needs of these women, I proposed activities which specifically addressed the area's weakness. Due to the genuine concern of those staff members who were more humane (some of them were replacements for those who quit following the lawsuit), I found remarkable cooperation at the upper levels of administration. In 1998, a shift of emphasis in treatment mode began to be discernible.

The process began with one volunteer reader — myself — and gradually expanded. Working with sympathetic and innovative staff, we put together a team to mentor the women in TEC.

My focus was to involve all the women, from the most withdrawn depressed to the paranoid schizophrenic. However, before I could teach other volunteers how to interact and behave under the unusual conditions the TEC unit population presented, I needed to gain the experience and know-how myself. My body language, tone of voice and demeanor were measured, bearing in mind the sacred need to avoid exciting or provoking fear in the audience. To hone my skills, I would go into the dayroom in the prison's high security Acute side and engage the women there; they might be suffering from delusions, hallucinations and/or depression. I would try to get them to express their needs, their wishes for interactions. I spoke with women who were just phasing off suicide watch,[15] who only days prior had slit their arms and legs nearly to the point of death. These were women who required extreme care and compassion, not judgment. Attempting to create a sense of calm and safety, I would gently read a story or share pleasant picture books, sometimes even drawing or coloring with them. This was the most challenging work I've ever endeavored to do.

Many of the techniques I utilized were bred from methods I had used working with behaviorally- challenged children when I was a volunteer at my son's school. Patience aided me in my inexperience, along with an indefatigable desire to reach out to the women suffering so much despair. It was trial and error, in part, but it was all carefully enacted.

The TEC women asked for books other than the children's books that were offered: books that were instructive or entertaining, with positive themes suited for them, so I searched for such books. Titles such as *When the Worse That Can Happen Already Has* and *Bad Things Happen to Good People* were substantial human stories for adults, telling of people who had been challenged but who survived and succeeded at creating a new life. These stories gave them hope.

Still, although they were enjoyed and were the source of continuing group discussions, they could also prove inappropriate. The mood or atmosphere in such a ward will vary; there was never a predictability of the unit's emotional tone. Before a group begins, a facilitator has to carefully evaluate the needs of the unit. We quickly realized that set agendas don't always work. Flexibility is part of successful mentoring or serving this (or any) population. They — the participants — need to control some of the activity's process and expression.

Other books were humorous or illustrative. The books acted as a point of common ground where positive group interaction could begin. Even the most withdrawn of women, in time, came to participate in activities these programs were providing. Pictorial landscapes were discussed, castles and other visual adventures helped to stimulate interest and give the women a pleasant fantasy and a chance to ponder other realities. Our attempts to pull them out of their world of problems and fears temporarily succeeded. We knew the limitations involved; we also heard and saw the great success we were achieving together:

---

15. suicide-watch requires constant supervision

laughter, songs, shows of affection, positive group interactions among women who never previously got along. TEC women were reaching out to others and supporting each other.

Expanding with Volunteers

As the time came to shift into an inmate team working with staff, we had to expand our formal structure. This meant coming up with a protocol and mission statement. After much conferencing and proposal writing, we were set to begin. The women were eager to participate; and I conducted interviews with potential volunteers, asking a string of questions:

1. Why do you want to go see the women in TEC?

2. Have you ever felt suicidal?

3. How do you deal with being falsely accused of doing something that you didn't do? (During bouts of paranoia and psychotic breaks, a TEC woman might accuse me of being a spy or a Nazi, and it was important not to take offense but respond with patient explanation, if needed.)

4. Can you separate yourself from the ego trip of a woman telling you she is in love with you? (On occasion, a woman would misinterpret compassion, or simply be lonely.)

5. Can you avoid playing favorites? (As a volunteer and facilitator, it is not acceptable to show favoritism. It is essential to not allow the TEC women to feel there could be anything beyond peer support. The women we sought to assist were vulnerable to acts of kindness and some, being accustomed to using their sexuality as barter for kindness toward them, needed to be protected. To ever exploit such women is an act of inhumanity.)

6. If one of your friends goes into TEC, are you prepared to say no, if she asks you to bring contraband in? (This is a sensitive issue. Loyalty to a friend in need is often the Achilles' heel to an inmate volunteer, and under the best of circumstances some contraband will escape detection. But there is a difference between a piece of chocolate and a razor. The extent of a violation would be determined by the character of the volunteer.) In this regard, we did not have any problem with serious contraband which could be used for self-harm. Self-harm was the only real issue of concern, as these women did not use weapons to attack others.

7. Can you commit to consistently attend your slotted days and times? (Due to the nature of this work, the TEC women needed a sense of predictability in their schedules and often lived their lives around our activities.)

8. Can you guarantee me that if you become aware of any dangerous behaviors or plans, you will let the unit sergeant or supervisor know, so they can

intervene? (Meetings with the supervisor and sergeant were held to reassure volunteers that problems would be worked out to promote a win-win outcome. A TEC woman who was hoarding pills would not be infracted but would be asked to turn the pills in; then her medications would be more carefully administered. In such cases, the TEC women wanted outside intervention and would use a volunteer to assist in getting that help.

9. Can you separate from your personal feelings about a woman convicted of a crime against a child, and serve each woman equally?

These were potentially major obstacles to confront for volunteer involvement. After answering these questions, volunteers also were required to agree to be routinely interviewed for quarterly reports, to avail themselves of debriefing services. Finalizing the process was the signing of the Mission Statement

An orientation was provided to allow volunteers to ask questions. I explained the program rules and purposes. That completed, I'd escort the volunteer to TEC and then demonstrate methods used to engage the women.

A book presentation demonstrated how to encourage the withdrawn to engage in interaction. Taking a beautiful picture book of fairies, dragons, horses, landscapes, whatever, I would say hello to the woman in the corner who doesn't talk, and with an innocuous question such as: "If you could meet a fairy, which would you choose? Or would you rather be here in this photo, with the wild horses running, or sitting inside this cave dwelling? I would pick this rock here, to sit on, because I could look at the flowers over there, see?"

Due to TEC restrictions, these women were never able to look at pictures in this type of book; they were prohibited, unless one of my team volunteers brought them in and looked through them with the inmates. Photographs and magazines were mostly non-existent until the Betterment work progressed and I obtained donations. We would make collages, cards, and picture frames, with cardboard, precut photos and glue sticks. The collages would have a theme, like "my favorite things," "beautiful dreams for my future" . . .

For each activity, we had methods to raise enthusiasm and camaraderie, both necessary for inspiring someone to identify positive aspects of herself when she is depressed. Gradually, in small increments, my programs expanded, from the one original children's book to inspirational adult biographies, humorous essays, arts & entertainment magazines, fashion magazines, photographic books of the ballet, pictorials of foreign countries, classical art, sculptures, and contemporary poetry.

Expanding the Range of Activities

By the time the program was in full swing, we were making poster art for display in the main institution (inspirational quotes), and we had a mural program, poetry reviews, music and dance, and a writing program that covered everything from writing essays and personal correspondence to assistance in writing legal correspondence and institutional memos, construction of crossword puzzles. The art program expanded to drawings in pencil, pastel, pen markers, and crayons, watercolors and acrylic painting, and creating cards and stationery. We also had group and individual discussions, watched videos together, and enjoyed some holiday visiting.

The art program began by just getting approval for white paper and a single pencil. After I proved no one would take it from me, we were able to graduate to using crayons and coloring books. From those sparse beginnings came poster paper, chalk, watercolors, and three paint brushes. When each increment brought no trouble, a set of new privileges was earned. At last, we were allowed to fill a basket with various supplies, and the volunteer would bring it in. All the items were also taken out and counted, afterwards, to be sure nothing like a brush was left in the TEC unit. This program later became a recognized success, and I began teaching the TEC inmates mural art.

The lawsuit filed by Columbia was still in the courts and as the legal battles went on and new staff took over, these issues were discussed openly with me and the security staff. I was allowed to voice my ideas and opinions as to whatever could be reasonably done to stop the escalation of self harm. More programs were permitted. A gardening time was allowed, and the women who chose to participate found it remarkable and wonderful. They had never been allowed outdoors to have recreation in the garden.

Amazing results began to occur. TEC inmates would tell me or another volunteer about a sharp[16] she had procured to self-injure, and would ask us what to do. Unit CUS began a rule that, in these circumstances, the weapon could be given to the sergeant or me, and it would not result in further punishment. Instead, the inmate would be acknowledged and respected for having reached out and stopped herself. Nothing like this had ever been formally tried. The lines dividing upper level unit staff from inmates and volunteers were put aside and we became a team, working for the common good.

TEC inmates began to build trust in the team of volunteers and staff, for the first time, to my knowledge. Laughter and acts of compassion toward others

16. A "sharp" is a piece of plastic, glass, metal or other object which can be used to self-injure

emerged; this was very moving. We women shared tears of hope and exchanged embraces; and held hands, as sisters. All of this was actually illegal and infractable behavior.[17]

When the music and dance program began, it was at times so much fun, the laughter filled the halls. We used a Karaoke machine and sang corny tunes that everyone knew. It was, at times, magic, and for a piece of time the tragedies and despairs were mere shadows. Even the shy might surprise us by belting out a chorus unexpectedly to the delight of all. It wasn't important to sing on key, just to get them to tap a toe could be a small miracle, and we were doing it, making small miracles. The majority of the women were on a variety of psychotropic medications (including monoamine oxidase inhibitors, which can make a person lethargic and tired), yet music can do things nothing else can. Physical movement was not greatly welcomed, but during our music and dance time, efforts were at times heroic and a gift to witness. To get some of these women on their feet and dancing was an enormous task, so with a little alteration we devised movements for those who had difficulty. They could stay in their seats and raise a hand and perform hand gesturing to go along with the lyrics. When a volunteer was assigned as music director, the women were delighted.

The work as a whole was not at all easy nor was it a pleasant job, though I managed to succeed where others had failed. I still had my share of objectors. Sometimes, when one inmate would get upset with staff for some trivial reason, the staff would retaliate by punishing all the inmates and cancel the program for that time slot. Some officers simply thought our work was not a good thing and considered it disruptive. In all things, there are those who resist change and progress; the work was for the TEC women, the sideline tribulations would just have to be endured. Most of the time, we had an uphill pull to achieve much of anything, especially after an arbitrary disruption by some staff member obsessed with trying to enforce the unenforceable had upset the whole place. The rewards were present each time a resistant woman would unexpectedly become engaged for those segments of time when her lucidity and mood allowed.

To push the limits even more, I explained how games could be incorporated as an educational activity. (The Betterment Program stressed education and pro-social activities). Astonishingly, the idea took off and we were able to expand our activities. We played cards, Scrabble, Charades,

---

17.Based on male institutional policy, physical contact among inmates is considered to lead to fights, and sexual assaults . . . to control this, rules against physical inmate to inmate contact began. When Washington State created its first women's prison, these same policies began being implemented in increments relative to the Equal Rights Amendment enactment. Unfortunately, female needs and expression are tactile and nurturing in nature. Policy does not recognize this gender difference, and women can be infracted for "displays of affection."

Pictionary, and did crossword puzzles, and I instructed the volunteers to allow the TEC inmates, mostly, to win (handicaps brought on by medications or illness left TEC's at a noticeable disadvantage). A success, even at nothing more than completing a game, raises levels of self-confidence and, as cognitive psychologists have shown, expectations impact a student. In fact, TEC inmates *were* students and the volunteers served as teachers.

R. Rosenthal and his research helped to guide my own theoretical propositions and my work with TEC, as I incorporated "the Pygmalion effect." I structured encouragements, instructing my volunteers to ensure the TEC inmates' success at their own expense — but not to allow one inmate to succeed at the expense of having another fail, when possible. I downplayed competition in the win-or-lose sense. Instead, I sought out wins for all. Certificates were one method to illustrate this. For a poetry contest, everyone would receive a certificate of excellence, each for her own unique contribution. Two women could not read or write, so I would give them a word such as "TRUE," and ask them to think of a word that sounds the same. They might say "BLUE," and I'd say what's blue? They'd say "SKY," so we'd have "True blue sky," then I'd ask what's in a sky? They'd say, "birds and clouds" . . . then I'd write it down "true blue sky, with birds and clouds." This would go on for a bit, and soon we had a poem. Their poem award might be "the best sky-high" poem award. No one was left out, even the Superintendents and others were recognized. After all, the whole purpose was to recognize and encourage.

Perhaps the best aspect of this "education" was that we had no standard, no curve, no grades except "Excellent," and no one failing to achieve.

Program Coordinator Duties

1. During my TEC involvement as Volunteer Coordinator the work entailed:

2. assessing TEC/special population needs

3. conducting interviews with inmates and unit staff

4. evaluating unit policy and restrictions

5. conferencing with the mental health CPM to establish ethical and legal boundaries (Dr. Michael Robbins, MH CPM)

6. identifying and articulating the goals of each activity

7. creating processes for security guarantees, and guidelines to monitor and conduct activities

8. purchasing and financial aspects

9. establishing criteria for volunteer applicants, training people in the screening process, distributing supplies, establishing unit admission protocol

10. proposal construction and approvals

11. distributing approved program specifications in completed form with copies to all parties: MH CPM, Superintendent, Assoc. Supt, TEC CUS, Sgt., and the State Attorney General's Office

12. beginning training and implementation

13. coordinating and monitoring programs for compliance, and keeping officials informed (bimonthly conferences with TEC CUS and Sergeant, monthly conference with Associate Superintendent; compiling and distributing quarterly reports.

10. Inmates' and Families' Needs

Reviewing the comments and requests made by 300+ female inmates during POCAAN, AVP, and TEC Betterment Workshops and seminars, several common issues stand out. Representative examples collected from January 1998 to August 2000 include:

- "I can't say no."
- "I can't trust women."
- "I'm not very smart."
- "I know I can make him change."
- "I would make him hit me."
- "I took the rap for my man, cause he would have had to do more time than me."
- "I love my kids more than anything, but I just couldn't say no to him."
- "I was molested when I was a little girl."
- "I haven't told anyone what my mom's boyfriend did to me."
- "I'm not as good as everyone else."
- "I never had a dad."
- "I don't know what's wrong with me, but I can't stop taking drugs even though I know I'm going to die from it."
- "I'm fat, and I hate myself."

These have been recurrent themes in the workshop activities since the outset. We therefore made it an urgent priority to present our lectures in a way

125

that would convey useful new attitudes, skills and tools to help the inmates with their issues relating to setting boundaries, to co-dependency, abuse, self-esteem, communication, and dysfunctional thinking.

Case Study — TEC Resident Annie

Annie was born and raised in Tacoma, Washington. She is 41, African American, and is housed in TEC. Annie and her four siblings were raised by their mother, whom Annie describes as a "drinker that liked Crack." Annie's mother died from cirrhosis of the liver while Annie was in prison. This is the third incarceration for Annie, although she has been arrested ten other times — mostly for prostitution and petty theft.

Annie hears voices and experiences flashbacks. She reports that bad men did nasty things to her when she was a little girl. One of these "bad" men regularly haunts her and orders her to do things. Some of the things she has done at his insistence is to rub toxic cleansing chemicals on her entire body; she developed chemical burns, which require medical care.

Annie functions at the cognitive level of a four- or five-year-old child. She has a tendency to do things like washing her hair in the toilet bowl, or refusing to shower for days at a time. Needless to say, her peers shy away from her for the most part.

"I don't wanna do no more Crack, this time. I wanna go live with my brother and his wife; but they got kids, so . . . Hey, do you have any tobacco for me? . . . Ow, my legs are hurting again."

Why do her legs hurt? "Cuz my mama told me bout the rats. I always cross my legs real tight and keep um closed all night long so them rats can't crawl up inside me." Asked to elaborate, Annie whispers: "You know, they crawl up between your legs and eat your insides. It'll kill you."

This fundamental misconception is not a unique example; it illustrates a level of ignorance and misguided beliefs prevalent in some sub-cultures of our society, in particular — or, at least, most important — with regard to female anatomy, never mind the basic behaviors of common wild life. Annie was given a simple lesson on female anatomy, and it was explained to her that mice and rats would be unable to survive inside the human body without access to open air to breathe. Another woman believed the vagina was a large bag, the length of her arm. She didn't believe there was a separation between the uterus and vagina. She believed she could lose a tampon if she inserted one inside her, and she lived in terror that one day something would get stuck inside her and cause her to die.

Annie is a typical example of the long-term residential inmate of a TEC unit. When Annie is in a regular general population unit, her behavior often causes unrest and agitation in others.

Some of her problematic behaviors were specific to the common cafeteria. Having finished her tray of food, she will go from table to table asking strangers for whatever food is left on their trays. Annie doesn't care if she is insulted; she only concerns herself with the food in question. On occasion, she will follow people to the garbage area where the trays are scraped off before being stacked for the dishwashers. Seeing the food thrown in the garbage can, Annie will reach in and eat from the garbage.

Annie chain smokes and consumes coffee with sugar and cream with equal vigor. When she runs out of her supply, she will approach anyone at all, and repeatedly request some of theirs. It is difficult for Annie to accept a "no," which irritates others around her. She has been repeatedly cited for an infraction for taking the cigarette butts out of the ash trays and smoking them. Annie has a very short attention span and her memory is impaired to such a marked degree that she will frequently forget a conversation within seconds. Unfortunately, this lack of short term memory is misperceived as rudeness by others.

Women from her hometown community say that she was not always as she is today, but Annie has a long history of substance abuse. Crack cocaine and alcohol were her drug preferences.

During the 20+ months Annie was an active participant in the TEC Betterment Programs, her behavior changed notably, in the following areas:

• Verbal communications increased from asking for tobacco etc. to actual recall of some of the day's events, brief stories about her brother, and comments about music personalities.

• Physical conduct altered. She began to sit at the common tables with others, rather than sitting alone, as had been her pattern. Eye contact increased.

• Earlier artistic work was limited to coloring children's coloring books with crayons. She progressed to conceptualizing and executing her own drawings. Annie graduated from crayons to pastels and finally to acrylic painting.

• Reading and writing were two activities she showed little, if any, interest in initially. Gradually, she became interested in the performance we created as part of the TEC Betterment Program's work, and showed a desire to participate. From being a mere spectator, Annie became a poet and public speaker. A great achievement was when Annie wrote a three-sentence poem and recited it before an audience of peers and staff.

● Emotional expression altered from yelling outbursts to more socially acceptable displays, indicating a degree of patience and willingness to work and listen to others.

Annie's participation in the group activities emerged in a slow progression, from twice a week to daily participation. Even on the three occasions (during the 20 months of the TEC Betterment Program) when Annie was restricted from participation as punishment for failing to complete her unit's janitorial obligation on time, Annie would return to full participation when staff allowed

Case Study — TEC Resident Barbie

Barbie, a Caucasian female, was born in the State of Washington at Western State Mental Hospital, where her mother and father were living as patients. Her parents were deemed incompetent and Barbie was signed over to the state. Barbie was raised in a series of foster care placements alternating with stays in mental hospitals. Today, Barbie is 40 years old; she was recently released from TEC segregation.

She reports a juvenile record for runaway, theft, prostitution, and assault. This is her second incarceration in prison following countless stays in city and county jails. She has no residence and has lived in the streets as a homeless person for most of the last 30 years.

Barbie says her mind runs away so fast, she can't catch it. She has difficulty hearing others and responding to them. When Barbie wants to have a cigarette, she will howl for attention, demanding permission to smoke. Barbie believes that she is "crazy" because she inherited it from her parents. That's what "they" told her, all her life.

"I don't give a f— just give me my check and a joint, a big fat joint and big fat c— to f— and s— and I'm crazy, oh, yeah! . . . ha hahahahahah!"

Barbie is a relentless joke-teller. She can remember dirty jokes from years past, which she repeats constantly to anyone who will listen. When Barbie is not joking, she is angry and screaming for either a cigarette, a cup of coffee, candy, or to be allowed to watch the TV. When she does mention her past, it is in short vignettes that are in no particular chronological order.

During a one-on-one, she was permitted to speak with me outside and to smoke. She related the following:

> "The cops said I got four years cause I got no home. I gave this guy my check to buy me a joint and he gave me ten joints for my check so I couldn't get no place to live. When I saw him again I was pissed and he gave me some rock

cocaine but then the cops busted me and I don't even like that sh—, you know?"

Barbie functions on the cognitive level of a five- or six-year-old child, on a good day. When she has a temper tantrum (which is weekly), she will defecate and urinate on the floor. Using her hands, she will spread her feces on the window, doors and walls. She sometimes refuses to wear clothes and even during her menstrual cycle she will bleed all over herself, refusing to shower. Barbie's chief complaints are that her requests to smoke, drink coffee or watch TV are ignored, and that makes her angry, so she retaliates the only way she can.

To force Barbie to comply and not "cause trouble," staff use force, and mace spray, to overwhelm her and place her in five-point restraints. Later, after she begs for mercy, she is placed in a segregated cell with no books or any other items she can use to distract herself — or injure herself. Barbie has a long history of self-injury, in incidents ranging from cutting on her body with a razor to scraping on her skin with a piece of plastic.

Barbie was an active participant in the TEC Betterment Programs for 20+ months (excluding her trips to Western State Mental Hospital and SOC Special Offenders Center at Monroe Reformatory). Her behavior grew somewhat more controlled, but these changes were of short duration: three-week periods. Barbie appeared to have cyclical bouts of acting-out, and it is conjectured that hormonal changes may be in part responsible for these monthly episodes. Improvements included:

• Enhanced verbal communications and ability to talk about her feelings while she was feeling them, rather than impulsively acting on these emotions. This shift showed some potential; more time in pro-social activities with guiding mentors could prove beneficial.

• Physical expression. She showed a substantial increase in affectionate contact with facilitators. Barbie regularly walked up with open arms and gave me firm embraces and enjoyed being near me.

• Artistic expression. Her activity was tentative, initially, and limited to coloring in children's coloring books. Twelve months into the programs, Barbie became obsessed with painting murals and it became the highest point of her social activity.

• Reading and writing were difficult for her due to her extremely short attention span; however, she did write some poetry and enjoyed having others read it in front of an audience.

• Modified emotional expression, from intense anger displays to excitement and laughter. She responded very well to positive feedback.

The Parenting Instructor's View

The program results spoke for themselves. What was most difficult was the situation for mothers with children. This issue is explained by Ms. S. Schmidt, WCCW Parenting Instructor. Ms. Schmidt earned an MS in Education, specializing in Childhood Education Studies and Adult Curriculum Writing. She provides WCCW inmates with a full program of six individual classes and a bimonthly Parent-Child Lab that allows "students" to interact with their children in a crafts-and-playroom type of format. Each year, 20 mothers and 10-20 children participate.

In an interview, Ms. Schmidt was asked to offer an assessment of the needs she has identified in her students during her four years at WCCW. Here are some of her observations.

> The majority of women here have histories of some form of abuse. In my work I emphasize self esteem. Self-esteem is extremely important in breaking the abuse-cycle, because-if these women had self-esteem prior to coming here, they would not have been as vulnerable to relationships which are abusive. This isn't to say that all women here came without some self-esteem; I'm referring to those that have abuse histories that were relationship-oriented and tolerated. Women with high self-esteem generally escape abuse; they won't tolerate it if they recognize it.
>
> Childhood abuse can be a factor that sets up a young girl to become a woman who later accepts abuse as an adult. It is the acceptance of abuse.
>
> The basis of my teaching is to help the women feel good about themselves. Some of the ways I do this are by providing them with opportunities to be creative. I provide a variety of class projects for them to choose from; mostly, these are simple paper, glue and colored marker-type crafts like the things their own children create in their schools. The mothers make them and then we display them on the school walls with the more adult-theme brainstorming work I have them do. The adult-themed work is generated by group discussion and then individualized; these can be their thoughts on family safety issues to ways in which they can express parental love.
>
> I've found with histories of abuse, especially in childhood, that the child's drive to achieve is broken. Giving my students opportunities to create something and then display it gives them not only self-satisfaction, but also validation that they do have valuable thoughts and skills.
>
> My own history as a foster parent brought me to this work with the women's prison. My household took in over two hundred and fifty children, mostly with histories of childhood sexual abuse. One of the parts of helping these kids is to allow them to express their emotions; like the women here, they need to be heard. This is part of building self-esteem. If you can assist in the

130

building of a student's self-esteem, as an educator, then as a mother she will better be able to avoid abuse in the future and be able to pass such skills on to her children.

A child or mom who has high self-esteem will not give into peer pressure, cults, or abuse relationships. That esteem gives you the power to say no when peers may offer you drugs or to do something against your values.

For me, I want to stop child abuse; so how can I personally intervene? I tried a lot of things to stop abuse, but you have to do it *before* the abuse. I approach my parenting classes with the hope to intervene [early], especially with the pregnant women. I care about the women here and I like them. I think they want to know about better parenting skills; many have said, "I could do better."

What scares me to death is, if they don't change their lifestyle, they'll come back. They need a mentor, someone to assist in providing them guidance when they transition out. It's so easy for some people to make money through drugs. They have kids who are used to having expensive things. These same children can put pressure on their moms when they leave prison, with expectations that mom will buy expensive items for them again. When a mom leaves here, she'll be doing well if she finds a full-time minimum wage job, to survive. She'll have to have two jobs; she won't be able to buy the Nike shoes anymore. I see a need for intervention to teach these kids — you can have either mommy or the pricey things, not both; or mom will wind up back in prison.

Regarding the needs women have at WCCW: education. Any educational class or workshop is going to advance them. The teachers here all show a tremendous amount of positive caring; the public doesn't see that, unfortunately. In my view, the graduations the women have here should be publicly broadcast, showing their achievements.

Mothers need to participate in the classes and the Parent-Child lab. They need the place and opportunity to bond. Visiting rooms are artificial because of the limits. The caretaker is there with the mom and kids, so the child's attention is divided.

When moms go to class and then the Parent-Child lab, it begins the process of establishing and changing methods and actual behavioral interactions between the mom and children.

Some moms think they are spending time with their children if they go get a video and put it on the TV. They need to learn how to play with their children. However, you can't expect someone who has been raised in a dysfunctional and abusive home to automatically know how to parent well; in these cases, you need intervention.

My students are active in their own learning; I engage them in the process of education.

New Roads To Rehabilitation — Is the Mother Always To Blame?

Studies have shown that an infant's ability to form healthy attachments later in life will be directly related to the earlier experiences of attachment formed with the caregiver. John Bowlby showed (in his famous "attachment theory") that without healthy bonding a child will be unable to empathize, and will behave with impulsivity and self-centeredness. This can give rise to a reckless disregard for the rights and feeling of others, which shows up as part of a conduct disorder and is considered the precursor to adult sociopathology. But is all this true? More recent studies have revealed that the "mother" is not necessarily to blame. A child's genetic disposition and temperament are significant in this behavioral puzzle,[1] and there is growing evidence that events a "good" mother might never know about can make all the difference.

Jay Giedd, a neuroscientist at the National Institute of Mental Health (NIMH), has conducted studies using MRI scans from which he now surmises that "impulsiveness, the disregard for consequences, and the rapid and unexpected storms of adolescence may be in part related to the immaturity of the frontal lobes of the brain." His work is discussed in Richard Restak's book, *The Secret Life of the Brain.*

The good news is that science has shown that the brain is plastic, in the sense that it keeps growing — it can change, even in adulthood. The organ's capacity to change allows us to adjust to conditions in a process of adaptation and recovery. However, plasticity is most evident during infancy. Growing cells interact with their environment and with each other. Neurons, newly formed, create bonds and connections which multiply.

Through our experiences the foundation for these bonds are established, and these connections transform into circuits. The brain changes when we change the experience — experience is literally that powerful. Brain plasticity continues throughout an entire lifetime, so that new pathways are continuously being built within our neuronal circuitry. However, traumatic experiences can cause some of these pathways to be destroyed and other strong new pathways may be built in their place. Experiences and behavior can affect the circuitry that develops in the brain, and the circuitry later determines patterns of conduct as we go through life.

Only the motor and sensory centers are nearly mature in early childhood. The prefrontal lobes continue to develop throughout the 20s, possibly even later. During the adolescent years, with immature prefrontal lobes, our brains have not firmly established the self-control or braking system needed for successful adult

---

1. Belsy, Hsieh, and Crnic, 1996; Fox, 1992. Seifer et. al., 1996.

relationships. If a child or teen experiences trauma, then uses drugs, alcohol or other "anti-social" responses to self-medicate and calm the fear centers, changes in the brain circuitry begin. Whatever succeeded in relieving the terror of the moment is "wired in" as a necessary response, should any situation trigger recollections of the terror. Such changes may alter behaviors or create new behaviors uncharacteristic of the individual. If addiction begins during this highly suggestible time, further behavioral changes may be developed — to cover up or pay for the addiction, for example. Substance use is no longer a choice, in the usual sense.

The immature prefrontal lobes do not yet have the moral dimension or sense of personal responsibility integrated (neuronally circuited) into the personality. Substance use and abuse cause neurotransmitter disturbances. A surge of dopamine within the pleasure circuits far exceeds the dopamine levels derived from a normal feeling of success, such as winning a game or competition, or any other natural physical experience. This enormous dopamine surge transmits the message to the brain that "this is ecstasy, this is rewarding and important." This pleasure-center experience is so profound that it builds neuronal circuitry within the brain. (And whoever is with the child during this phase or high may become an important part of the picture, an association built into the memory.) That new circuitry creates an overwhelming desire to repeat the experience again and again. Steve Hyman, director of the National Institute for Mental Health (NIMH) explains that "All addictive drugs are Trojan horses that mimic natural neurotransmitters."[2] They fool the brain-reward pathways and signal the impulse to find more drugs, it becomes compulsion.

Because of the shape and functioning of the brain changing, with some circuits strengthening and others being pruned out, this substance abuse can rewire the pleasure responses by drug associated electro-chemical firing of the reward pathways of the brain. With time, the brain becomes wired for the pleasure associated with drugs, and the anticipation of obtaining more. This drives the teen to focus on those people and events associated with the drug experience. Due to the depth of this pleasure center recording/encoding, past pleasure center records of say, the birth of a child or the love for family, has now been usurped, or at the very least is now under intense competition.

With this intense craving, foreign behaviors may begin — such as lying and stealing — creating a personality revolution/transformation. Moral and behavioral lines are crossed and illegal acts begin. Activities that go against her moral code occur, and the person begins to become estranged from her former identity and former relationships.

---

2. Restak, pg. 85

Anna Rose Childress, a psychiatrist from the University of Pennsylvania, specializes in drug addiction treatment. Evaluating PET scan recordings of addicts, she discovered that when addicts viewed videos of cocaine-drug associated activities, "a clear signature for desire" could be seen operating in the addict's brain.[3] Another study of cocaine users showed patterns of brain activation in the neural systems normally seen in social attachment being replaced by a cocaine-induced euphoria. Where patterns associated with the voice or image of a loved one occur, the cocaine high replaced the area with its image.

If love and cocaine can exchange brain tenancy, this helps to explain why it is so difficult to break the addiction. It is not merely moral "weakness" that causes 80% of those addicts who undergo treatment to relapse within six months.[4]

Studies of chronic addiction are just beginning to make headway in this promising area, and new therapies are being developed.[5] But much more work is needed, and victims and those who wish to help them still have a long road ahead.

A Community Leader's View

Frank Kinney is on the Prison Superintendent's Advisory Board, which provides representation for the community in dialogue with the institution. Kinney is also treasurer for Rebuilding Families, a non-profit organization in Washington State founded on the belief that women inmates can rehabilitate themselves. Rebuilding Families seeks to cut back the returnee rates of WCCW inmates. Its main goal is to reduce recidivism; it also helps children of inmates avoid a criminal future. To those ends, the group organizes programs to support family bonding for inmates and their relatives, provides mother-child resources, and generates opportunities within the institution and beyond into the community.

The programs involved in this effort are:

A). The pregnancy and infant unit in the Minimum Security Compound, one of only three in the country. The pregnant mother is allowed to give birth and keep her baby for up to 18 months.

---

3. Restak, pg. 88
4. Restak, pg. 88
5. See Gerwe, Corinne, 2000; *The Orchestration of Joy and Suffering — Understanding Chronic Addiction.* New York: Algora Publishing.

B). The Greenhouse Program. Inmates take horticulture classes and receive accreditation. These skills are then implemented in an actual greenhouse which provides wholesale service to local retail shops.

C). Mom and Kids Volleyball Program. Mothers and the caretakers of their children are able to have a monthly three-hour visit with activities and shared refreshments.

D). Girl Scouts Beyond Bars. Mothers meet with their Girl Scout daughters monthly for a scout meeting and organized activity. Lunch is shared and the mothers are trained to be Girl Scout Leaders for the program. Transportation is provided by a licensed Girl Scout community leader.

Frank Kinney is passionate about helping the children of inmates from becoming future statistics, future inmates. He believes the intervention these programs are providing not only gives the mothers assistance but, by reuniting the children with the mother in positive programs and a more natural setting than the prison can provide, creates an opportunity for these children to be mentored and guided to follow a different path than crime.

On Wednesdays, Kinney provides pastoral care. He says,

> My main purpose is to keep the children of these moms out of crime. If God gave me one wish, it would be to see not one child come here, later, as an inmate. For any of these programs to work, the moms have to care enough to keep themselves on the right track. To expect them to do this alone is wrong. A lot of women come here and find a relationship with God, and it is real. The Christian groups come in here and help bring them into this fellowship. They support and care and pray for and with these women.
>
> The problem is, our work has stopped there. When it's time for the mom to get released, they say good-bye and she reaches the streets alone. No more support system, no more fellowship and caring friends. She has kids, they have to survive, she'll sell her body before she'll see her kids go homeless, or sell drugs; whatever it takes.
>
> My work is just starting to address this community void, to look for support. Churches must come to see that they need to be there in the communities for these women and children when they're reunited.

Kinney is 77; he has been actively involved with the inmates of WCCW for over 14 years. He has been to McNeil Island for men, also. When asked why he is so driven to help this segment of society, he stated:

> In a nutshell, my father wanted my mother to get an abortion; she refused, and I'm here. Seven incidents in my life occurred where I should have died. I've committed my share of sins. By 64, I had ruined everything: my marriage, my

life; and I said, 'Lord, where do you want me to go?' I've been here for 13 years. We all make mistakes that could have landed us in prison. Some get caught, some don't. We have these kids left behind. We have to protect them so they don't experience the backlash of public prejudice. Other kids can be crueler than adults. Of course, the mother needs to do her share in this work. It's a cooperation process.

In discussing the current societal attitude I've defined as crimiphobia, and why it's so prevalent today, he said:

> The male cry from my generation has been, "I want my kids to have it better than I did." As a result, we gave it to them, so much that we robbed them of the tension that provides the opportunity to learn how to cope with life. We provided too much for them.
>
> So many said, after their kids went bad as a culmination of this over-providing, "I just don't understand; why are our kids this way?" No parent wants to admit they did all they could, and they did it so good they may have done too much.

In regard to why he is focused on women, Kinney concludes with a fervent message.

> I love children. The responsibility of having the child really falls on the mother. She bears that responsibility while pregnant, while giving birth, and while nursing and caring for the infant. She will raise the child, when she is released from prison. If we can give these moms self-sustaining skills, learning lessons to help them enter society, then there is hope for the children. Rebuilding the families starts inside the prison. We need more men to get involved, more churches to assist. We can't keep leaving them at the front gate. We need to provide positive, supportive transition into the community as well.

The Children Left Behind

Protecting the children involves protecting the mother: In 75% of homes where there is spousal violence, there is also violence against the children.

Gavin de Becker compiled a list of warning signs for mothers to watch out for in partner relationships. Some of the particulars are when the man:
- accelerates the relationship, and seeks commitment too fast.
- uses intimidation and verbal abuse; uses threats and actions to control others.
- abuses substances, and uses that as an excuse for behaviors.

- has a police record and history of battering relationships (whether reported or not).
- is paranoid, inflexible, jealous; controls money.
- projects extreme emotions onto others without due cause.
- minimizes abuse, identifies with violent characters.
- won't take responsibility for his problems.
- exhibits mood swings.
- includes weapons in the power concept he utilizes.
- shows double-standards and sexist attitudes.

Children who have experienced abuse prior to and during a mother's incarceration can be helped to heal.[6] Part of this process entails helping the mother to take responsibility for her choices and then allowing her the opportunity to work with her children in validating their experience of fear and violation. This gives children recognition of their worth and value. This "witnessing" and accounting for the child's experience is essential.

As of 1998, an estimated 200,000 children in this country had mothers in prison. This number has steadily increased. Over the last 20 years, the female population increased by nearly 400%. The male prison population went up by only 200%. Most of these women have at least one child who is a minor. The disruption and trauma these children will and do suffer is made often worse by the lack of contact with their mothers. These children need opportunities to work through their losses and to prepare for reunification. Because the mother will be the child's primary caregiver when she is released, work must be done to help create healthy bonds between them and to establish parental behaviors which serve the child's best interest. This must include opportunities for mother and child to interact beyond the formal and unnatural visit room environment.

Ultimately, by successfully treating the mother's drug addiction and healing the fractured family, the criminal justice system will reduce recidivism rates and the child welfare system will preserve and reunify more families.[7]

Toward these ends, both systems have a common interest in 1) providing opportunities for mothers to plan their children's care, to maintain and build relationships with their children, and to help their children heal from the trauma they experience; and 2) encouraging mothers in jail to live sober lives and develop new skills that will enable them to cope with the pressures of living in their communities and raising their children.

---

6. *The Drama of the Gifted Child* and *The Untouched Key*, by Alice Miller.

7. Excerpted from the Special Issue on *Children with Parents in Prison*. Many useful links and resources are provided by the Child Welfare League of America at CWLA [online], at ‹http://www.cwla.org/programs/incarcerated/›.

"I do not understand the legal system at all. I thought its purpose was to protect and serve yet, by incarcerating women just as harshly (in some cases more harshly) than men, it is breaking down families. By nature mothers are the nurturers, protectors, and teachers to the child. Most families are single parent and by remanding the mother and removing the nurturer and teacher, then who is left to guide and teach the young which is the future? The child is punished the most, then society — because the children are the future and by their mother being incarcerated it affects them emotionally, mentally and physically. It's a domino effect." (AA21)

"Being a woman to me means having: self-respect, self-control, morals, boundaries. Taking care of my child, being a nurturer, teacher, protector, role model, having a career, goals, dreams, strong, independent, educated, loyal." (AA21)

A woman these days must be strong — we carry all the burden. Society treats women at a lower level because it's still a "man's" world. Us women have struggles only a woman can relate with. (C10)

We can reduce recidivism in this hidden and silent population if we listen to their voices. Family is a key to rehabilitation, and healthy relationships are required if the goals of Corrections are to be realized.

11. THE SURVEY

In addition to participating in and leading programs brought in by POCAAN and others, I conducted a survey of women inmates to test their attitudes, self-awareness, needs and concerns, and to elicit suggestions that could be fed into more productive and effective educational programs within the penitentiary system.

From April 3 until April 30, 2001, my volunteers and I conducted interviews. Most women completed the questionnaire in about 40 minutes, sitting with one or two friends at a dayroom table. Two had the questions translated into Spanish. Some of the responses were highly charged. One woman, upon being asked to respond to a survey, blurted out, "The women need to take responsibility! They made the choice to commit a crime." She got no response, and shortly left the table where the others and I were seated. Another said, "If there were places different than prison, those women could learn new skills to say 'no,' and how to create boundaries, so they could recognize what personal responsibilities are all about. Wouldn't that help better than prison as we know it?"

Some of the respondents were self-conscious, because they could not write or read very well; they hesitated, until I explained that I would read and write for them. Others were somewhat uncertain how to respond to the questions — the answers were difficult to find. To the initial question about abuse, they would say, "Well, no, it was my fault," or "I don't talk about that part of my past." Then, on another level, it was, "Yes! Yes! Yes! It happened to me, and it hurt me; it wasn't fair."

When it came to, "What has helped you the most" — they were baffled, and couldn't think of a thing. I offered some possible candidates: classes, here? Church? Lover? Nothing? Then, they usually came up with something.

The overall reaction upon hearing about this study was curiosity, and then agreement to participate. The women were intrigued to think that anyone would ask them for *their* truth, their opinion. They were so familiar with a system that dictates to them and classifies them based on their category of offense, that the opportunity to experience having their side of things recognized was refreshing and welcome. Some remarked, "I hope this will help others," and "Maybe someone in D.O.C. will read it and they'll make changes."

The questionnaire began with a caveat — "You do not need to use your own name and can refuse to answer any questions." I expected the majority would invoke the right of anonymity; they did not, and their consent was given to use their full name and DOC number with their answers. When it came time to make the results public, I assigned the respondents ID numbers anyway, which simplified the task of tabulating data as well as providing a level of privacy.

The 138 survey responses reflect all segments of the population at WCCW.

Survey Respondent Demographics	
Race	
Caucasian	77
African American	29
American Indians	10
Hispanic	8
Asian/Pacific Islanders	5
"Other"	9
Age	
Oldest	53
Youngest	18
Median	33
Crimes Convicted	
Violent offenses	69
Nonviolent	34
Drug-related	22

No response	13
Education	
Some college	14
Graduated high school	21
GED	35
Some high school	57
Some junior high school	14
Drugs/Alcohol abuse	
Yes	111
No	20
N/A	7

Crimes were not identified beyond violent or non-violent (although many respondents gave details, anyway). Only 6 stated that they were innocent. The crimes of conviction went the full range from arson to child abuse, burglary, kidnapping, delivery of drugs, assault, murder, and embezzlement. Most said they had a history of abusing alcohol or drugs.

And while it may not be surprising that many of the women who find themselves in prison have a life history that includes being abused, a full 136 of the women surveyed (99%) said that they had the impression that their friends at WCCW had a history of abuse; 10 said they had not been abused, themselves, and 6 did not respond to that question.

Interviews with staff were conducted during break times and totaled approximately 30 minutes. We took notes, wrote their comments, and submitted the results back to each interviewee for final approval.

In-depth case studies were conducted over several weeks during non-working hours. Various documents, official and non-official records were used for clarification of particulars regarding the women's crimes of conviction. The average in-person interview lasted approximately five hours, and the write-up was presented to the participants prior to entry into the final record.

The responses did coalesce around certain basic points, as I have indicated throughout this book: three of the most glaring issues were their lack of knowledge about women's health issues, desperation at being separated from their children, and a sense that they had not been ably defended and were not able to make full or proper use of the legal system on their own behalf.

The humanity expressed by the women, and their urgent desire to mend their lives, comes through in their words. Not surprisingly, some reflect a certain naivety about how easy and satisfying life could be. Others seem to have few illusions; still, they look for something positive to grab hold of, and strive to build a future while courageously taking responsibility for their own actions.

While generalizations are always hazardous, a sampling of survey responses reflects the general background, mood, and current aspirations of the women in Washington State's women's prison and will serve to sketch a collective portrait.

***

The Questionnaire and Representative Responses

Question 1: Do you have any experience with abuse?

a) Do most of the women here you know have histories of abuse? Yes /No

b) Has sexual, physical or emotional abuse changed or affected your life?

c) Has abuse influenced your choice to commit a crime?

d) If innocent of crime, state so.

e) Did abuse cause you to react to life instead of thinking out your behavior first?

- Yes. It changed my whole life, because of who had abused me. I lost all respect for any authority figures, such as my mother, father, uncles, grandparents, teachers, etc. (Yes) AA3

- I do not think I stopped and thought of crime or to commit my crime as a choice. — I committed my crime more because I didn't think. Not innocent. CM

- I am here for my husband's crime. He was given less time, put the blame on me. He doesn't speek any english. NRI

- The crime I am currently incarcerated for, I am innocent of. However, I have been involved in criminal activities for the last 10 years (all of which have gone unpunished) and I do feel that the various abuses that I suffered as a child contributed greatly to my thinking patterns, which led to my life of crime and drug abuse. Therefore, yes, I do believe that abuse changed and affected my life and caused me to react to life rather than act, based on careful thought. C9

- I believe that emotional abuse has had a very big part on my choices of crime. I sought love and attention in criminal activity. My mother emotionally abused me all my life. C12

- Yes. No. My addiction changed my life's path. AA14

- Yes. Because I suffered sexual abuse as a child. I believe that made me more inclined to accept both physical and emotional abuse, in adult relationships. Because of my shame, guilt, and very low self-esteem, that led me into numbing everything with drugs. Drugs and fear of the person I was with is a major contributing factor to my criminal behavior. C 13

• Although sexually, physically, and mentally abused and being in a hospital being reconstructed at the age of 9, I've never felt compelled to take and abuse someone else. Yes, I've got 1,100 pages of transcript says I'm innocent. C5

• I am innocent of the crime I was accused of. Yes, because my abuse started mentally, then it was physical, then I became my worst abuser mentally and toward others physically. AA15

• Yes, it changed my life path. . . I know that if I would have had no type of abuse, my life would have been different. However, the things I have endured has made me into the person I am today. 6AI

• As a child, I was sexually molested until I was about 12 or 13, on and off. Just touched. Yes, it's changed my path in life, I hold things inside a lot ("stuffing") and really couldn't express my feelings towards anyone. * NO, it doesn't involve anything pertaining to this crime. A/PI3

Question 2: What are the most personally satisfying activities you do? (visits, positive friends, sleep, eat, whatever. . .)

• The single most satisfying to me is helping people of a less fortunate nature. Such as the mentally challenged and people who have locked themselves into a shell.

• 9 times out of 10, it is people like this who are extreme victims whose innocence has been taken in one or more forms. C4

• Working with rescue dogs (dogs we rescue from the Humane Society); painting, drawing, and learning new things about myself. CM

• Listening to music. AA26

• Visits, school (parenting classes), being sober, reading.

• Talking with friends at church and school. H3

• Working out, school, drawing, visits with kids and family, spending time with friends. H8

• Hanging out with friends, working in the Braille program, and going to school. A7

• Activities I like to do here? Reading, playing cards, sports activities like volleyball. Out there? Dancing, hanging out with friends, shopping. A/PI3

• Prayer. AA25

• I recently attended the 4-day Kairos retreat [a Christian-oriented 3-day event], and that was probably the most enriching experience that I have had. I also attend a weekly counseling group, promoting positive change, and that has had a significant impact on my, as I am learning to come out of old beliefs that I had/have about myself. I also write constantly. I have always had a very hard time communicating verbally, so writing has always been and still is a form of release and survival for me. C13

• I find NOTHING about being here satisfying. C2

• Read and write and play cards. And being there for someone when they need me. AA22

• I have a group on Fridays that is very enjoyable to be with, playing cards. And associating with all the different kinds of people and observing the way humans as a whole work. AI2

• Reading inspirational things, visits from family. A/PI4

Question 3: If you had a college degree, how do you think it would change (or would it?) your attitude, image of self, or your criminal behavior? If you are innocent of crime — still, explain how a college education could impact your life.

• If I had a college degree not only would it boost my self esteem but it would give me a head start on accomplishing my goal to be a social worker for youth at risk. C2

• I am a black, a woman, a felon and a Muslim. That in itself gives me so many strikes against myself. I will be incarcerated for 8 years before my release. When I get out the job market will be very competitive and I will be at the same level in which I came in at — 8 years prior. Having a college education will prepare me to be able to be a productive citizen and I will be able to provide for my child without having to resort to criminal or immoral behaviors. C14

• If I had the patience and the money to get a college degree, yes — it would change everything about me, for the positive. However, it would have to be something I was interested in. 6AI

• By boosting my self-esteem I believe to some degree I would have more self-respect for myself having more self-respect would detour me from self-destructive behaviors. AA21

• It would make my self-esteem more positive and I wouldn't have to turn to my old criminal habits to survive. A7

• I believe I would have a greater dimension of thought patterns, and a way to fulfill my time adequately. 4AI

- I would probably think more of myself as a person. A college education would give me self confidence as far as getting a good job. And with a good job, I don't think I would act out criminal behavior. But who knows? 5AI

- It would help me be more independent. AA27

- I was usually a straight-A student. I believe that having a college degree could have been, or made, a big difference in the way I saw and felt about myself as a whole, thus maybe keeping me out of criminal activities/behavior and drugs. I am counting that now, as I still have a lack of belief in myself, but somewhere inside I know that there's a lot of good qualities in me. And I am worth having an opportunity upon my release to be able to financially support myself and my children. Because of this strong desire to improve, I am currently attending an 18-month cosmetology course here, and plan on obtaining my license upon my release. Just knowing that I am committed to this and am applying myself has aided in my personal-worth feelings. C13

- It would prepare me for the challenges of life and keep me out of trouble. AA27

- I don't think having a college degree in itself would change any of that, wholly. As for criminal behavior, it can be heavily associated with the type of crowd one is involved with and a college degree may make the need for monetary crimes less likely. But not all crimes are committed with deductive reasoning and logical thoughts. So, No! CM

Question 4: What do you think the public thinks about you, and why?

- I believe the public thinks I'm a felon with no heart who doesn't deserve a chance in life. That's the impression I got when I was released [the first time]. C1

- I strangled the man who molested my children and I don't care what anybody thinks about me, because I know who I am and what I stand for!!! A19

- I think, based on the recent court decisions and lobbying being done, that the majority of the public sees me (as a convicted felon) as being not worth saving, unredeemable. It seems like people do not realize that I am human, intelligent and no different than they are. I just made some bad choices and want another chance. They don't think of me as a mother, a daughter, a sister, and a worthwhile human being with something to contribute to the world. I am not a number. C9

- I think the majority of society thinks I'm deranged, because of my case and why I'm here; but also I believe that the other portion that knows the entirety of it does not condemn, but understands. A/P12

- I believe they think I am a bad person because I have been in prison. People don't get to know you, they judge everyone the same. When filling out a job application if you check that you have been convicted of a crime, 9 times out of 10 you will not get an interview. The stigma behind being in prison is everyone is bad, can't be trusted, you get what you deserved. They don't stop to think what may be caused you to commit a crime. C74

- I think the public, well most of the public, see or think I'm an innocent teen who's life has been robbed of them, the other half of the public probably thinks I'm a harden criminal with no chance of change or to be a real American citizen because of the crime I was convicted of. H7

- The public groups convicts, and judges all inmates, by the male inmates' recidivism and reoccurring crimes and actions. C8

- Negative, stigma of what goes along with being gay, the life of crime. What's to balance out the criminal behavior? Balance of good vs. criminal life. There isn't enough to show I can build houses. C 15

- I think they believe I'm way too old to be robbing and shooting heroin. Why? Because I am. C2

- The public probably believes what the media leads them to believe and therefore I feel condemned. C35

- They (those who don't know me on a personal level) think I'm a monster because of media misinformation/lies. C66

- I think the public as a whole is sick of crime and violence. They don't look at us as individuals; they look at us as a whole that is a burden, financially, and have no place in their community. The families of the victim think with wounded and hurt emotions. Probably think I should be executed. Public's opinion gets harsher if they have personally been affected by crime. CM

- I believe the public believes I am just another troubled teenager who should be locked away for life, because I got locked up when I was 15 for first degree murder, first degree assault, and first degree burglary. I believe society doesn't want to recognize us youngsters for who we really are because that way it's easier to lock us away and throw away the key. If I was given another opportunity at freedom, I would never go back to crime. I've realized how precious freedom is and I would rather be homeless than to commit another crime. C70

• I guess maybe they think I'm not good enough to fit in out there. And they see me as a failure, because of my past, with getting into trouble all the time. 4A1

• Right now at this point in my life, it doesn't matter what the public thinks because I'm not trying to prove anything to them — only to myself. A7

Question 5: What has helped you here the most? What do you need, that this place hasn't helped you with?

• Seeing my children and being able to hold touch, see and let them know I love them. Without my children I'd grow cold and hard and empty inside. C35

• The superintendent denied my right to have trailer visits with my oldest daughter because my crime was considered domestic violence due to the fact that it was my daughter's father who was strangled to death in my crime even tho we were never married. So my answer is more personal contact like trailer visits with my oldest daughter. Two hours in the visiting room is not enough especially when I have 5 more years of incarceration left.) A19

• Getting clean and sober. Getting my GED — something that I would not have gotten on the outside, running the way I was running. But most of all was getting to know the real me, and getting in touch with my higher power. AA14

• The things here that have helped me the most are the school programs, the Toastmasters, and the "clean time" that has allowed me to get to know myself, as I really am, for the first time ever. What I need that this place has not provided me with is treatment for my drug addiction and mental and emotional problems. I am not eligible for drug treatment due to the fact that I have "too much time left to serve" and I am not a "DOSA" inmate. I am not eligible for intense therapy because I do not have a court order for it and I want therapy, not medication. This is discriminatory and unfair. C9

• What has helped me here the most is the life skills class. I've built a lot of self-esteem and began to truly believe and not give up so easy, it gave me lots of hope. I don't believe it's the place it's you. You have to want to change because there are a lot of programs that can help you if you want to help yourself first. C12

• The vocational education has been a good help for me. I need more education and more help, with outside resources for support. AA26

• This place has helped me to start healing from the abuse I had in the past. I still have a long ways to go to heal. I think that one on one counseling is a lot more better than groups in here. C7

• What has helped me here most? Well, I can say that being here hasn't really did anything for me, I had to fight for an education because I was only 16 years old when I got here but I have had a lot of encouragement and support from the inmates to become a young woman with accomplished goals and lived dreams. What I think this place should offer? Programs. What's a G.E.D.? They also need more guidance programs for younger offenders. H7

• I've completed the full course in Life Skills. I need the proper medical attention for the disease of Hep. "C" and I have not been getting proper medical attention. A14

• The things I feel that this place has not helped me with is my addiction to sell drugs. This is my second time here. I am 24. I was first here when I was 19. I've been selling drugs since the age of 10. There are treatment programs for users, but not for people like me. AA3

• Being totally involved in numerous programs definitely attributed to my growth, my spirituality, programs such as AVP, Life Skills, Domestic Violence, CD, MRT, and adult basic education helped to give me a sense of self worth and value. C56

• My job with the prison Pet Partnership Program. The ability to deal with the fact that I don't know how to place the internal guilt that I feel about my crime, nor some way to feel less pain and give back to society more. CM

• Learning. My brain, when not in use, turns to mush. I could better myself if only I had access to more education. C67

• I've wrote to a lot of battered women's organization and they have helped me to "de-program" and have given me information and support. A/P12

• Getting clean and sober. Getting my G.E.D. — something I would not have gotten on the outside running the way I was running. But most of all was getting to know the real me and getting in touch with my higher power. AA14

• The time that I've been here has taught me and showed me not to take advantage of life because it's precious. When you've never taken the time to dig down in yourself and really know what you're really worth sometimes it's not until you're locked up that you really get to know yourself. What do I need? LOVE. AA 15

• The thing that has helped me the most here is getting in touch with my spirituality. The time I have to think, ponder and study and practice is the only thing that has helped in changing my thinking process. This place has done nothing to aide in my rehabilitation. At most it has helped in destroying my self-esteem. It has made me resentful and angry. They have done nothing to address my mental health, and other abuse issues. Their answer to my problems is to medicate me. This place is supposed to rehabilitate me yet I am deprived of any real education, beyond a G.E.D. or office training. I mean really, do you think I'm gonna come out a better person when I'm constantly being put down and treated like I'm less than a human being. I'm not receiving adequate education and instead of giving me some therapy or one-on-one counseling I'm just being medicated. I need mental help and an education and some positive reinforcement to leave here successful. We need more through self-help courses. AA21

• Just being here has helped me to clear all the drugs out of my system. I've only been locked up 4 months, but I'm actually starting to feel normal again. A15

Question 6: What are the reasons that would make you go back out and commit a crime?

• If I didn't have the support system I now have here. This is another area I believe they try to destroy. Many of the women are sent to Pine Lodge in Spokane when all their family is here. Ten chances to one the visits stop because of the distance or are few and far between. C74

• No support, no money, loss of my children, drugs, no education. CI

• If I don't learn other ways to live and make a living. No educational opportunities and lack of drug treatment would definitely increase the chances of me committing more crimes. C9

• Same neighborhood, same people. AA22

• To get the things I need to survive: I would go back to crime before I would go homeless or let my children go hungry. AA14

• I would only do another crime to defend myself — like if my ex-husband came after me to beat me again. C7

• I never had a criminal record until now; back home we have judges, prosecutors, lawyers, and law enforcement agents in the family. I did not commit this crime. I will not return to a life of crime. C5

• For me, there is no reason I could come up with that would be good enough for *the choice I made* to commit a crime.

- No skills to get a decent-paying job. AA26
- The inability to support myself and my children is the only thing that would lead me back into committing another crime. The crime would be selling drugs, as it is always a money guarantee. I think that after I successfully complete "Cosmo," I know it's a real fight to get approved for a state license, even if you score very high on the state exams, because of being convicted of a felony. I also know that employers are scared to hire convicted felons. So, I am attempting to prepare myself for the difficulties I will be facing so I won't have to rely on old behaviors. C13
- Nobody caring about me when I eventually get out, nobody willing to give me a chance and give me the benefit of the doubt, lack of opportunity, etc. C4
- Loss of my family structure, my income, running into a lot of others b.s. about me being in prison and gay. So many obstacles that I would revert to what I do best, drug dealing. C15
- I could not think of a reason to commit a crime. Going out of prison must be terribly hard. I feel that something inside my soul changed after I realized what I had done. Even leaving with nothing could not force me to break the law. CM
- Someone molesting my kids or hurting my family, sister, mom, brother. C29
- If I continued to use drugs. AA25
- Coming out with a "label" where as I came in as a person "society" would accept, hire, work with. A12

Question 7: Do you understand the legal system?

- No. A7
- I believe Washington State has a complex legal system, also that a lot of the agencies here have problems following laws made by the Legislative bodies. I would say I do know the legal system, especially since law has always played a role in my life and education. C5
- Yes, I believe I do. 5AI
- Not really. AA26
- I do not understand the legal system at all. I thought its purpose was to protect and serve yet by incarcerating women just as harshly in some cases more harshly than men. It is breaking down families. By nature mothers are the nurturers, protectors, and teachers to the child. Most families are single parent and by remanding the mother and removing

the nurturer and teacher then who is left to guide and teach the young which is the future. The child is punished the most, tan society because the children are the future and by their mother being incarcerated it effects them emotionally, mentally and physically. It's a domino effect. AA21

• No. They say one thing and DO something else. Plus, my attorney took the easy way out — she steered me into a plea bargain, which now I know I could have beat. She didn't do any background work, because she didn't want to take time. AI

• Now, I understand all my rights and the law — back then, I knew nothing and didn't understand. A/P12

• I don't understand this legal system at all. CI

• I understand a little about the legal system, the law and my rights. But I know more now than when I was out there. A/P13

• No. I do not and there really is nothing to help us understand. We have the law library, etc., but if you are not well educated in the first place, how is that gonna help? A12

Question 8: What is wrong with the current prison system? (Your ideas of what would really help you.)

• The current legal system stinks. It doesn't treat women right. We are way different than men and we shouldn't be treated like them. They need a whole new different system for women for prisons. They need to do more intensive research and come up with a plan to rehabilitate women period. New system, definitely. AIP13

• Sentencing guidelines. Educated and unbiased staff. A/P14

• Not enough programs. Men have way more drug programs such as educational and vocational. WCCW has sh-- to offer and then for some courses or privileges the qualifications to join are ridiculous such as no minor infractions history. When you have pigs here that ??? on you and write you up. Inmate's word don't mean sh-- unless we're accusing each other. A/P14

• I think the system needs to focus more on the reasons why women commit certain crimes and proceed to help women understand why they react to situations the way they do. Need to show us how to change inside so we will not stay in the same thought mode. The system needs to provide more vocational training for women. C72

• They don't see that guilty by association is not right; men do less time for the same thing and women are the home makers and care takers and in locking them up for long terms takes all that away from their children not enough schooling giving children too much time. AA8

• A man does less time for a same crime as a woman because there's an "image" that the women shouldn't do crime, they should be Betty Crocker. C8

• I believe the current prison system is over populated with women who have ridiculously long sentences, and it's understaffed with people unfit to do their job. C I

• I think when you are 16, 17 to 25, you should go to some type of a work camp, mentally, physically challenging, cooking, building, relationship skills, classes in communicating with others, one on one, people act different in groups. C 15

• It's racist! Staff lies. Favoritism. H4

• I think that most of the staff employed here are cold, and unable to see us on an individual basis, for who we are! The health care is totally what I consider leaning toward the dark ages, as it is very hard to obtain treatment when needed, and it takes so long to be seen. C13

• They are biased because women are still viewed as homemaker, men are treated less for the same crime, when sentencing comes it don't work, it is unrealistic for average people. C 16

• It doesn't allow or exercise on the internal instincts, emotions or overall nature of what is in a woman's natural make-up. We are emotionally and internally different from men and they need to not only recognize this but allow us to show and exercise these god-given qualities! C4

• The prison system does not really understand how women are different from men. Some of the C.O.s (male ones) try to be verbal bullies and for some women that have been abused this is hard to deal with. Also I feel there should be more activities for the women inmates and their children even the adult children. C7

• The prison system stinks. They don't care what happens to us. What would help me? Well, people who truly care about what happens to me and what my future holds. More people who can relate in some way, better law actions. They need to do better background checks or scan, help people who need emotional, physical and mental therapy. Help those who need rehabilitation whether it is for drugs or any other addictions or physical and mental problems. Programs for women who have children after the prison gates especially for women have long term prison sentences and need a whole new start at life. H7

- Everything — they lock you up and forget that you're human. They don't feed you right and they treat you like you're nothing. Just because we're here doesn't make its any less human. We are still people with feelings and needs. Maybe more so, now, #8 Favoritism, snitches, liars, I. lack merit, abuse, harassment, invasion of my body (strip searches) pay system (income)-racism verbal abuse, threats from staff, control freaks, lack of medical care, dental, no rehabilitation, mental need mental help. No unity amongst women AA18

- I could say some things, but not on paper. CM

- Prejudice, favoritism, harassment, very disrespectful, bull head bullies, verbal threatening, counseling rehab full of sh--, also nurses, doctors need to get on their job stop sluffing off. AA 19

- The legal system in the state of WA is backwards. It doesn't understand or want to comprehend Battered Women and their mentalities-they automatically say that their temporarily insane. The prison system is no different; they order you psych meds but they have no information or "real" help groups. You're left to your own devices. Community supervision is a joke. It's only to make sure you pay fines or pee in a cup. AIP12

- I am innocent and my trial was based on all hearsay. The child (my daughter) was court ordered to see a child psychologist but C.P.S. and the prosecutor never took her. Now it's 10 years later and the daughter is fighting with the system to have the truth come out. She has had stuff in the court appealed for over 5 years but they won't acknowledge it. My public defender did a good job-but the prosecutor is/was dirty in ways. I come from a small town and a well-to-do family. C7

- What was wrong with the way my case was handled was: I tried to offer them information that they would really want — a lot more people my co-defendant has hurt by robbing them of credit cards and stealing from their bank accounts — in exchange for a shorter sentence or some of my property back. They weren't even interested. They didn't even have any idea how many more people he has hurt — but I do. I know their names, numbers, accounts, etc. C6

- Battered wife syndrome was not an option when I went thru trial-my Attorneys felt the abuse was a motive for the murder and didn't want it brought out. Yes, I had a Public Defender. Yes, they handled it different than I would have like it presented. C8I feel the system needs to branch more within its self Drug offenders have different needs than violent or sex offenders. Our counselors should not be paper pushers. The people who do our reviews should have to work more closer with us more of the time. Violent offenders who have long time sentences need to still grow emotionally, be understood and have an earned phase system so we don't get stagnate or hide in routine. C44

• I was not provided the chance to have professional witnesses. I was not allowed to have the witnesses interviewed by professionals nor face my witnesses face to face or enter any evidence that would have shown other evidence. C33

• Consistency with rules/regulations. Lack of due respect from officers (mutual respect), I'm stereotyped as dangerous because of my crime and not evaluated for my character. That's not fair to me as a human. C66

• Lack of medical care, lack of education; put some life skills here, for long-termers, better than what they've got, so they can put their life together when they're released. They need a positive outlook so they don't go back into abusive relationships — if they live with an abusive person, they are more apt to commit another crime. AA22

Question 9: What is your age, completed grade level; were you convicted of a non-violent or violent offense; alcohol or drug abuse history?

• I was 27 when I was locked up. I'll be 58 when released, LVN license from UCLA, Caucasian. Conspiracy to commit 1st degree murder — exceptional sentence given because I misused my place as his wife and misused his trust: 1 year for every year he didn't live. Men live to 72; he was 26 at the time. 46-year sentence given. Social drinker. Pain pills due to the physical abuse. AA14

• 34, GED and certificate in office training/computer skills, Native American. Yes: violent offense (murder, 2nd degree); yes, drugs and alcohol. A7

• 40, 11th grade, Black, violent crime, drug history. AA25

• 28, 9 + GED, White. Property crime, drugs – yes. CI

• I am 36 years old, I graduated from high school and have a G.E.D. I am a white female. I was cruelly convicted of first degree Felony Murder (by way of accomplice liability) and the only time I ever did drugs was during the 6 months I was involved with my co-defendant and boyfriend, who committed the actual murder for which I was convicted. The same man who stuck a needle full of heroin into my arm, for the first and last time. C4

• 36 years, 10th grade, Black/Indian. Drugs crime; yes. AA14

• I'm 33. 12th grade plus some voc ed. White. Violent. None. CM

154

- 29; 11th grade + GED and a little college. Japanese/White/Mexican. Attempted murder, 1st degree. Drugs & alcohol. A/PI3
- 34, 2nd year of college, Asian, nonviolent offense. Yes. A/PI4
- 51, 8th grade, White, violent, yes. C2
- 35, GED, African American, violent offender. AA27
- 27, voc/tech/college training, African American, violent offense, no drug abuse.AA26
- 33, 10th grade + GED, White, forgery and escape. I never had any legal problems until I ended up in an abusive relationship and with a man who used drugs. So my drug use led to my crimes. C13

Question 10: Define what being a woman means to you.

- I think "Phenomenal Woman" by Maya Angelou sums up the whole essence of being a woman. C36
- Everything, mother caregiver, so on. We have to work harder at change. The women in the sex industries have no programs to help change them and most of us are single parents. C43
- A woman these days must be strong-we carry all burden-society treats women at a lower level because it's still a "mans" world. Us women have struggles only a woman can relate with. CIO
- Nurturing, helping people, growing, taking care of people, being nice to all people, being understanding, being humble, coexisting the mentally challenged-less fortunate-and underdog. Getting people through hard times and through life! C4
- A woman these days must be strong — we carry all burden-society treats women at a lower level because it's still a "man's world." Us women have struggles only a woman can relate with. C17
- Being a woman to me means having: self-respect, self-control, morals, boundaries. Taking care of my child, being a nurturer, teacher, protector, role model, having a career, goals, dreams, strong, independent, educated, loyal. AA21
- A woman is loving, nurturing, caring, motherly, warm, gentle, beautiful. . . all the great things in life. They make the world — They're just precious. I'm happy to be a woman! A/PI3
- The nurturing part of humanity. The ability to create life; and having an inner softness.
- This is a hard one. To me, being a woman means many different things. As a woman, I feel compelled to meet the stereotypes set forth by society, antiquated notions of being a wife and mother before all else.

155

Trying to fit into a role that didn't work for me has led to a lot of confusion and pain throughout my life. I am now going through the process of discovering my own definition of being a woman. Ideally, I want to be strong, yet still be vulnerable. I want to find my own path, and then be led down it by one stronger than myself. I want to have courage, yet be protected. I want to nurture, and also to be nurtured. I am constantly searching for the perfect balance in all things, and eventually, I know I'll find it. C9

• A woman is a beautiful person who has great potential for success. AA26

***

Voices of the Inmates

A few telling excerpts from the longer interviews are included below, highlighting the need for counseling in prison and, by the way, indicating glaring gaps in social protection that contribute to the destruction of many girls and women.

Vanessa

"What is abuse?" Things that happened to me that I buried inside. I felt scared and angry — if a man was a bully, I had a hard time not doing what he wanted and that would make me even madder at myself. Kent was really nice but he was really mean, too. I did what he said, and I didn't like that. My crime was planned out by Ken, but I was also angry — because I allowed myself to put his wishes before what I knew was right and wrong. It was wrong to lie and manipulate Ms. Beard, and it was unforgivable for me to try and kill her. I was solely responsible for what I did and it makes me sick to my stomach. I don't have the words to explain the bad feelings I've gone through in dealing with it, except I could never do it again. I don't like hurting other people.

When I was brought back to prison, I knew no matter what, I had to unbury the things that happened before my crime, to move forward. That's what I've been doing. I know who and why I was angry at, because someone else helped me to talk about it, to feel it, to express it — and they believed me.

I would say that I felt like a pressure cooker — I was the pot of beans inside, and the bad things that happened to me were fire. My lid was on tight, so on the outside my pot looked normal, but inside I was building up anger over what was happening around me; yet I couldn't release the pressure because I didn't know how. Finally, my pot exploded and that young woman innocently and wrongfully paid the price of that.

After I came back in 1996, I took little steps at facing the truth; it was easier to blame Kent so I didn't have to look at my own lies — lies about me having everything together and being on top of my life. The reality though was I still had the biggest issues buried.

The most shameful things I hid were memories of things I went through when I was a kid. I had to relive my worst nightmares. Things I had buried so deep I never wanted to admit to anyone — I couldn't even admit to myself but a little at a time. I saw others do it, about their most shameful things, so it gave me courage and I didn't feel so alone and sick. Bringing it all up and feeling it and expressing the experiences was something I never did before, and it made me even more scared inside. I wondered sometimes if I was going to lose my mind, but I didn't. I was scared others would hate me and think I was dirty, because I felt that way. The weird thing is that no one did that. I received understanding and compassion — they understood. I learned that I was responsible for my bad choices but what happened to me as a child wasn't my fault. I figured that the men who did those things to me must have used the same lies in their heads to excuse the raping of a child — the same kind of self-bullsh-- I did, about my crime. There is no honest way they could rationalize their actions by saying that the girl set herself up for it because she ran away from home and put herself in that position, just the same as I could never again rationalize my actions by saying it was Ken's idea and that girl shouldn't have been out partying with a stranger.

That reality is so hard core to me that I cringe to write it. But the point is, and I can and I must be the woman I choose to be.

Kelsey

While at WCCW, I went to the TEC unit due to emotional problems caused by abuse while I was growing up. I was suffering from post-traumatic stress syndrome. I was having flashbacks and nightmares. I was basically reliving being sexually and physically abused. It was really hard for me to talk to staff members here, because I didn't feel comfortable.

Some of the girls volunteered to come down and sit with us. They didn't force us to talk but just made everyone feel comfortable, like they had a friend. They played games with us.

I really thought, at first, that I was losing it, when I went down there. After I was incarcerated, I was forced to deal with issues that I had never dealt with on the streets. I eventually opened up to one of the inmates that volunteered to go to TEC. I began to realize that I wasn't alone, and that I wasn't crazy. What I was feeling was natural.

Although today I am no longer in TEC, and still at WCCW, I feel as if I can honestly feel again, and can actually be myself. I am learning who I am, with the help of people who volunteered in the program in the TEC unit. There are also downsides of being in the TEC unit, too. You feel isolated from the rest of the population. You have to eat at designated tables in the dinning hall, and you can't socialize with anyone else. I know that I felt like I had someone, once I went back in Population, to talk to. Although I was only down there for 3 ½ weeks, it helped me realize that people can't stuff their abuse. It won't just go away. To use drugs didn't help, either. It only made me lose touch with how I felt and who I was.

— Kelsey

Tina

This was the most difficult of all the case reports for me, because of the circumstances in which I met Tina. It had been an especially difficult time in TEC, with one of my volunteers undergoing personal emotional problems. The volunteer herself had been feeling depressed, and going into TEC frightened her. We had discussed this and she felt she wanted to continue even though a staff at TEC had been the source of her anxiety.

The woman who worked as a correctional officer was cruel to the inmates and would antagonize them routinely. We had reported her misuse of authority, as had the TEC residents, but institutions have union employees and once they are in it's near impossible to move them. There have been longstanding problems in the restrictive units. Assignments at these locations are bid on and if you have the seniority you generally obtain the post you seek. A man who enjoys handcuffing and watching women undress can bid for a post in AD-SEG for example and then he will do hall checks and movement as part of his duty. The catch is that he can exceed his necessary checks and come by, peering in the door windows under the guise of a hall check and watch women on the toilets, or dressing, as he pleases. There are no areas of privacy or modesty.

It is also a given that those in AD-SEG or TEC are there because they are not "normal" or are "acting-out." Therefore, their allegations and complaints will often go unheeded. The staff know this and it gives them free rein to abuse their position of power. Do they all do it? No, but for the ones that do, the ones who don't will suffer the backlash.

The evening I met Tina, she had come into the residential dayroom where I had been doing art work with some of the women. Tina was tiny, in a waifish type way, her chin held down and pale skin gave her a vulnerable, sickly persona which also told me to approach her slowly — I did not want to frighten her.

I invited her to sit at the table beside me; I knew she had just arrived at the institution, because I had never seen her before. There was really no conversation with her during this first meeting; she was in shock and almost catatonic. I told her who I was, why I was there, when I'd return, and that I hoped to see her the following day.

The next day Tina whispered that she wasn't eating and couldn't tolerate anything other than fruit. From the dayroom table where we sat, we could see a paper plate piled with leftover fruit from the women's lunch trays and breakfast sacks. I knew the staff would often take the leftovers (and that is a good thing, rather than throwing out edible foods). So, I went to the door window. The problematic female C.O. came to speak with me. I explained that Tina wasn't eating, and she said "Yeah, we know. It's her choice."

I then asked, "Can't she have a few pieces of the leftover fruit? She said she'd eat that, and I'm worried, she looks very pale and weak." The staff gave me a look of disgust and said, "It's just a game. She's doing this for attention. She can't have anything but what's on her tray, which she refuses to eat. Don't play into her game."

I persisted. "But, if she won't eat the tray food and there's all that leftover fruit no one is eating, why won't you left her have some? She is obviously feeling faint and weak."

"This has nothing to do with you, Miss Compton, and you need to mind your own business." She turned and walked away.

This was not a new problem. I had on other occasions requested food for others, and other staff would give it, if they had leftovers from the inmates' fruit allotments or sealed juice containers. But there were always one or two that derived some sick pleasure from denying another.

Gradually Tina, seeing my earnest efforts on the women's behalf, began to lose her fear of speaking. Her whispers were so faint I could barely hear her, but what I could make out was that she missed and loved her children very much. That she suffered from some emotional trouble was evident and I wondered if she had a chemical imbalance.

As it turned out, the volunteer who was suffering from depression (in large part exacerbated by the female C.O. at TEC) also was able to bring Tina out and get her to talking. The volunteer and Tina began to form a friendship which appeared to assist Tina tremendously as the months progressed. Within a year Tina, was able to leave TEC and move to the medium custody housing unit. This move was a year ago and Tina has since done very well. The process of adjustment and growing "normal" Tina and I attribute in part to her stabilization on effective medications for bipolar manic depressive condition. What follows are Tina's own words, transcribed from a tape recording and a letter made specifically for this report.

My name is Tina Weaver. I'm here for attempted murder, second degree kidnapping and second degree assault. I'm going to tell you a little bit about me first before I answer the questions. Um, since I was 13, I was on the streets. Me and my Mom never got along, . . . you know, she abused me physically. My step-dad molested me when I was a kid, I have been raped, I have had the sh-- beat out of me . . . I have literally gone through Hell as a child, always wondering where I was going to sleep, if I'm going to get fed or not (sigh) [tape cuts off].

Well, actually as a child I overdosed. I tried hanging myself, I tried numerous times to kill myself. I've been at St. Pete's Hospital and Western State, Puget Sound, all of it . . . nothing really helped. Well, actually the only thing that helped is that I have four beautiful children and I love them soooo very much. Their names are David, Christopher, Rosalinda and Juan. I'm sure that they miss me, I haven't seen them in two years." [She takes a deep breath, clears her throat and begins again.]

Okay, I'll tell you what happened that day, I committed my crime. I had been to Western State (mental hospital — in-patient) and had been trying to kill myself so many times I had ended up in the hospital a lot, and I would get out a lot. Well, this time I got out and was staying out for a long time. I wanted to get my kids back and I figured that doing a visitation would be okay. It was on a Saturday and I took my kids to Discovery Zone and I let them play around forever, and then took them to Lakewood Mall, where they had a huge pizza, I can't believe they ate it all. Then I let the kids run around the toy that's in the Lakewood Mall and they were having fun when I called Lola (the children's foster care parent), the lady who has my children now, and I called her and asked her if I could have the kids a little bit longer; and she said No. Then I got really mad, because I didn't want to bring them back, and something inside me told me, 'Do not bring them back.' But, I didn't listen to it. I brought them back; and I was going to pick them up the next Saturday and keep them, you know. But, the last picture I have in my head is all four of them crying out the window, wanting their Mom. I should have took them that day, and I didn't. And then the next Saturday, Lola got a restraining order on for my kids because she said I abused them.

Cops came to the house; detectives came to the house. And each one of them said my children were not abused. I couldn't even get a statement from CPS because there is nothing there.

At this time we're going to court and the judge, well at this point I didn't know what I was supposed to bring, so the judge tells us what to bring for the next time. So the next time I have everything that I need but he wants more — my twins were eleven weeks premature and so they had physical therapy once a week. We went to the doctors so many times because they got ear infections and all. I got a statement from them and from my best friends but the judge didn't even want it, and that was the third time going around.

I was confused. I was lost. I was hurt and boy was I mad. I just couldn't-I didn't know why this was happening to me — I wasn't thinking very good. I had quit taking my medication and I feel like I didn't care anymore, not about my kids, I mean my life. There wasn't anything there without my kids.

What I did because Lola kept my kids, she has a daughter, Laurel and she's retarded. I went to her house and told Laurel to come down to my motel room because her mom was going to be there and we were going to talk about getting my kids. Which was lie, but she did come down there to the motel with me. I offered her some pizza she ate two pieces, she was real hungry and I gave her some soda and I let her watch what she wanted to on T.V.. I didn't know what to do next so I taped her to a chair with duct tape . . . which after I did that.. I looked on her face and she had such an empty look to her (long sigh) then I called Lola and I told her I had Laurel, and I was threatening I was going to (barely audible) kill . . . her. (Long pause and sigh). A few days before this I went and got me a gun and I got the bullets. At this time I had already yelled at Lola's answering machine that I was going to kill her and she called the cops. The cops come to my door and they try to unlock it but I'm holding the lock so they can't unturn it, cuz I didn't know what to do I was so scared. And the gun was in the hall and she was sitting in the chair, she was duct taped pretty good, but by the time I wanted to stop and not do it anymore the police were at the door. And I got arrested. I have been in jail almost two and a half years. And I haven't seen my kids or talked to my kids or anything like that. I also don't have anybody on the outside. My Mom, I don't know where she is.

[Tape cuts off, then comes back on.)

The question was: 1. Has abuse physical, sexual or emotional influenced your choice to commit a crime? Did it change your life path or are you innocent? I'm sure not innocent. But yes it has affected me, the way things are right now because of the abuse.I got physically and emotionally and sexually abused. I been molested, . . . and I have been raped. I have literally been through Hell and back. I put myself in that place you know, even though I was a little kid. Except for the fact, I . . . I . . . my step-dad molested me for a year and a half when I was in Germany. And I couldn't say anything, you know what I mean? I couldn't tell my Mom. She wouldn't listen to me, she never listened to me. She didn't even like me, she really hated me. And she'll tell you that too. Right to our face she'll say, 'I didn't even like her.'

That's okay, I love her half to death. But, as a child, I couldn't let my feelings out (sigh and deep breath) and when I said no to people, everybody just ignored me. And when I tried to talk to people, they would just ignore me like I was talking to air.

And about this time in my life, I want to have someone to actually listen to me, what I was wanting to say. So I wrote letters saying I was going to kill Lola and I um . . . on her answering machine and stuff, which I am not proud of, but she could have given my kids. I had a place to stay and I had a roommate and there was no reason the kids could not come and live with me. They even told the guardian *ad litem* they wanted to live with me — but as it usually happens, nobody heard me.

I can scream at the top of my lungs but nobody will pay attention. Everybody says, 'but, your voice is so soft', but when I'm yelling at you, how can my voice be so soft? You know, listen to me. I can't make people listen to me enough. When they start listening, they get on another subject. Things are really f--'d up nowadays, aren't they.

The second question: "What are the most personally satisfying things you do?" When I was in Germany, when my step-dad was molesting me, I was a little klepto. I stole everything. I mean you had it I had it. Which I don't do anymore. Anyway I was confined in my room and during the summer, the both summers, I was always grounded to my room. During the summer, it was for a month, I would look out my window and I would watch kids play. Just watch them play and eat ice cream — whatever they did, all I would do is watch them. I enjoyed that. My Mom didn't like that, every time she caught me she tell me to knock it off, but. . . . Yeah, I was grounded for months, not weeks, not days, but months. I still watch people out my window. I'm not spying; I just watch. But this time I can go outside and be with everybody. But for me, my personally satisfying thing is to sit on my bed and watch what people do, see how they act, all that kind of stuff. I enjoy that very much.

3rd question: "If you had a college degree would it change your attitude, your self image, behavior?"

I'd have to say yes to all of them. If had a college degree and was going to school and not paying attention to guys, I wouldn't have no children, I'd have a life. I wouldn't have kids that were running underneath me, you know. I'd have my own place, I'd eat what I want. You know it's just a dream to me anymore. I'd also have a better outlook on life and everything around it, cuz like you know I could — well if I did go to college maybe somebody, just maybe somebody, would listen to me and I wouldn't be a nobody.

4. 'What do you think the public thinks about you and why?' I think the public thinks I'm a nuisance, I'm not worthy to be around, I am behind bars. I committed such an awful crime that I should be locked up for a very long time. Some people will understand, we all make mistakes this is just a very serious mistake. People will always tell you there is always a way around it. But, I'm here to tell you, that there is no way around it. Sometimes you are just stuck, no matter how hard you try.

Question 5: "What has helped you the most while in prison?" Well, the prison has activities and I really enjoy getting involved with them; Body Pump (an exercise program) I also really like it when I can feel comfortable around my roommates and friends. I don't have to put up a front so that they'll like me. This is what I have in here they may not be friends but acquaintances but sometimes it helps to have someone to lean on.

Question 6: "What are the reasons you would go back to crime?" This is my first crime that I have ever done, besides speeding, but for what it's worth I do not care if I am homeless. I do not care if I am hungry. I don't care if I don't have anything in this world, I will never in my life do something stupid in my life again. I don't plan on coming back at all. I have to change my life, it has to be changed in order for me to go back out into the community. Who knows you might go out and come back you just don't know right? Well, no. Not me, I am not going to give anybody any reason to come at me like that, okay.

Question 7: "Do you understand the legal system?" Not at all. I do not know what is right or what is wrong. I hear things from lawyers I hear things from friends and things from inmates. . . I am totally out of it. I don't know anything about this legal system except it put me away for 24 years. I'm not saying I didn't deserve that, because what I did was very wrong — I have never been in the system before and he didn't want to answer my questions or when he did it was a one word answer, I was like going crazy. But as always I am always pushed to the side and nobody does listen, even when I cry.

8: "What's wrong with the prison system?" To be honest with you, I don't know. I don't know what to expect. Of course we have to keep ourselves in line and of course they are going to help us do that whether you want to or not. You eat what they cook you and as long as you stay in line and don't act stupid or retarded, you know, it's fine.

9: "What is wrong with the way your case was handled?" First of all, I got the worst attorney possible. His name is John Chin; you don't want him. I was getting mixed messages different people were telling me stuff and I didn't know who to believe. I basically screwed myself because I didn't understand that if you go to trial I'd get a chance of not having to be locked up so long. He told me "No, you'd probably get more time." So I took the plea bargain. I did not get any paperwork from my attorney until I got to prison and requested it. As like everyone else, John Chin listened to what my crime was and he just didn't care. But what do I expect from him, he's just a lawyer.

I also tried several times to get different attorney; we just didn't see eye to eye and each of those times I asked him if I could get a different attorney, he said no. Everyone else told me no, that that I could. And then in the court room John was telling them stupid things I did and he told the judge that I had a knife and I was going around to each room and that Lola saw the knife and then I dropped it. First of all, that story was a dream I had, that I told John I had. I never did that. I had told Lola about the dream, too, and she had said it's okay to have dreams like that. But I was scared sh--less in the courtroom and I was standing straight, you couldn't even move me if you wanted to. I was so scared, I couldn't even talk to tell them that, no, it wasn't true, it was a dream, it never happened. But, I was too scared; I couldn't get it out. It was all so new to me.

Question 10 says, "Your age, your grade level, your race, crime and do I have a history of drug or alcohol abuse?" My age is 26. My grade level is about ninth. My race is white and my crime is violent and I'm really not proud of it. As a kid I started doing drugs since I was thirteen years old my choice was crank and weed. As a little kid I used to shoot up and I was constantly high. I even overdosed a few times. Well, I can safely say that I will not do any kind of drug besides my medication. To me, that's just going down hill and I'm trying to go up hill. When I was a kid, people would buy me beer. Can you imagine a thirteen year old shooting dope in her arms? I don't do no more drugs and I'm trying to keep my head on straight. The medication I take is Lithium, cerylquil, Wellbutrin, Trazadone and Visteril. My eyes are hazel, my hair is brown, I'm 5'6 and I weigh 129. I love my kids very much and I hope one day I might be able to see them again. That's just wishful thinking.

Number 11: "Define what being a woman means to you?" Being a woman means to me that people don't take you seriously, basically. They look down at you, they look at you like you're dirt. You have to work harder for your money and you're always second, like what I did. I was cooking cleaning and shopping taking care of the kids, that's what I think of other women too. But some of the women who went to college didn't have this problem. Guy listen to them; guys don't look down at them. But, us drop-outs, they sure look down at us.

[Tina later gave me a letter to add.]

I wanted to let you know that I realized something about myself. As I mentioned before, I was a klepto. I was living with my mom. I was 11 or 12. I remember a time it was after Halloween I snuck in the kitchen and stole some cookies. My mom caught me. She sat me down at the table. The Halloween candy was in a big silver bowl. She made me eat all the cookies and then I had to eat the candy. I got so full that I threw up all over my hands. My mom made me lick my hand (fingers). I kind of know why she did that. She got so tired of me stealing, so I guess I had it coming.

When we were in Germany, my mom would yell at me for getting up from bed to go to the bathroom and she'd say "hurry up and get your ass to bed." Even before she locked my door, I could go to the bathroom but I got scared. So, there was a box in my closet. I went and peed in that box. My room started to stink. I had a dirty laundry basket and I peed in there, too. I'm not proud of it, I just want you know the truth. I wrote a note that my mom found. It said I wish I were dead, at 11 or 12 years old. She slapped my face. I don't think it would bother her too much.

Also at that time, my step-dad was molesting me for 1 1/2 years. When my mom found out about my step-dad, he got arrested. Me and my brothers and my mom came back to Washington. Again at this house I was afraid to get up at night and I started to pee on the side of the bed, on the floor. She found out and of course punished me. My mom also made a blanket into a diaper. She put it on me and made me go outside where my friend was. In a way, it was my fault and I deserved some of it, but not all that. I went into a foster home because she couldn't stand to be with me. Can you blame her? But I can't blame her, I was a real bad kid, no kidding. After foster care, I was all over the place. I ran away from wherever they put me.

I was at a friend's house and I said, The hell with it. I don't need to live. I mostly caused trouble. I found a bottle of phenabarbatol for seizures, about 30 in the container. I popped all of the pills. I woke up in the hospital. They said that I had quit breathing a few times. They put me in a mental institution at Fairfax. When I got out, I went back to the house and overdosed again. Again, I almost died. I went back to Fairfax. When I was in Puget Sound, I tried to hang myself but I got caught. And only a few years ago. I was an adult and I kept on taking sleeping pills again and again. I just didn't care if I died or lived; my children were living with Viola. I was so depressed, I just laid on the couch, no TV, no radio. I would watch when the sun went down. I saw the shadows on the wall, I scanned my phone calls.

I don't know how long I was like that. Then the war starts with Viola. She got a restraining order so I couldn't see my kids. When I was first arrested, they put me in Western State offender ward. I refused to eat. I also tried to hang myself again. I wanted to get caught (not at first). They had to restrain me, I was kicking and yelling. I was not on any meds, I refused them. At jail, I finally gave in and took Depacode, Celexa, and Trasadone in the 4E medical unit in jail. All I did was take my meds and sleep. Then I quit Depacode because my hair was falling out. Now they put me on Lithium, Seraquel, Visteril, and Trasadone.

I am looking at myself. I was not okay. Who yells for no reason? No wonder. my kids were hard to take care of. Now I'm in prison. I take my meds. For awhile, I even cared for Ms. Shumway (an Alzheimer's patient). I care for myself, also. I know I am a beautiful person. I'm kind and I care too much about people. I always share my stuff, but then when I go to get something, it's gone. I can't complain. I used to hate to read, but now I can't put down my book. When I did my crime, I wanted my kids back anyway I could. I'm not that monster everyone saw. Yeah, I hated myself, that poor lady was so scared. I wanted, at that point, to stop, but I didn't know how. Then I was a monster. That lady will always remember that I hurt her. I told her I was not going to hurt her or her mom, I just wanted someone to listen. I am disgusted with myself that I did that to a person. Normal people don't do stuff like that. I am so sorry that I did my crime. Not because I got put in prison. I hurt that lady, but also, I haven't heard from my kids in 2-1/2 years. Things work out, so I guess I deserve what I got 24-1/2 years. But that lady, I hurt for a lifetime. I know now I had a few loose screws. I look back and I, I remember how I felt.

There was something wrong with me. People just don't scream for no reason. Why didn't anyone notice that I felt out of control? I was not stable. My mind didn't think right. My head is screwed on now and I haven't felt this good in a long time me. Besides the fact I don't have my kids, I've hurt someone for life. I'm content with my life now. I have a great roommate and I can look around the pod (A) and I realize no one here hates me. And don't forget my honey, Vicky. So yeah, my head is clear, clear as glass. I like my job as a janitor and I like to go to school.

When I was a kid, I hated school because it was just so hard. My mom told me to write the spelling words 50 times each word, 20 words. I would flunk my test. I flunked spelling, math, English, social studies, and reading. The highest I got was a C+, maybe one B-. Now I do great. A's, B's, and only one C+. When I missed a word after writing them 50 times, I had to go to 100 each word, 20 words. And believe it, I would get some wrong. I tried really hard not to act like my mom. My mom would make me do dishes everyday and I did that with my oldest.

I love my children so much, it's just not fair that I can't see them. I don't even have pictures of my kids. My life has not been easy, but I'm trying to make myself a better person, to leave the past (never forget), but put it behind me. I have a great future ahead of me. Maybe, just maybe. I would love to see my kids, I miss them so much.

Each of my kids have a meaning to their name.
— David Michael: I have two brothers, named David and Michael.
— Christopher Alan: I have a good friend Chris.
— Rosalinda Marie: She's my only girl. Rosalinda is a beautiful rose in Spanish. (twin Juan)
— Juan Antonio: Juan is named after his dad (Rosa's twin)

Cool, huh?
This is me, my life, my thoughts, and my actions. None of this should have happened. I made the dumbest decisions in my life and I hurt so many people. I'm sorry for my life, but not my kids.

I wrote this to add. It has a few things you might want to say. Yes, all this is true. But it wasn't only my mom's fault or anyone's fault. I can't push the blame on anyone. I was a bad kid, and that's why my mom reacted to me stealing. Not all was okay, but some was me, if I were a good kid, maybe none of this would have happened. Please don't judge me for my crime; I'm not that person, really.

***

Tina says that her days in TEC were hard because she was still getting her medications adjusted. For her the TEC volunteers gave her hope that she really could make it and that she could make friends. The activities helped her to focus on something positive and not dwell so much on her problems.

Today, Tina has made a turnaround in her life. She is enjoying a sense of accomplishment and can see her past weaknesses, she said:

> "Tell them I realize now that I wasn't prepared to have my children back full time like I thought I was. I feel so much more aware and in control of myself. I've finally got the right medications and I feel normal. Imagine what my life could have been if I had been on the right medication out there, you know — I never would have done my crime. Isn't that something?"

12. Recommendations

Educational Design

I gained a very broad exposure to the population at WCCW and their concerns by working as a tutor, a lecturer for chemical dependency groups (STOP), a peer counselor with POCAAN, and a Lead Facilitator for AVP. The recurring complaints and the voiced needs of the female population revealed a consistent set of primary problems (summarized in Chapter 8). Fiscal limitations, however, meant that there was an enormous disparity between the women's needs and the available programs and resources. The operational therapeutic groups lacked the necessary depth of examination, and opportunities for long-term penetration of the issues in question simply could not be achieved. Band-aids were supplied where wounds required major surgery.

Independently, I set out to construct programs which could potentially serve these areas. A framework was developed to guide the work, specifying that the participants would be responsible for
- Working in a social context
- Exercising decision-making abilities
- Gaining a critical understanding of the rights and responsibilities of self and others, and how these elements are needed to mutually co-exist in society

- Developing an attitudinal predisposition to make decisions within a wider range of options than previously realized, when matters of choice arise
- An acceptance that with self-change comes the expectation and advancement to serve as a peer role-model
- For peer facilitators, to act as "agents of change"
- Utilizing the humanities to help themselves transform into responsible, critical and productive citizens.

The fundamental principles established in the internal framework of these programs were intended to meet the personal desires and needs of the group, while simultaneously answering the expectations of society by fostering pro-social behavior and increasing the probability of:

1. behavioral citizenship, which supports its society
2. personal and community responsibility, adhered to by its members individually
3. self-empowerment, self-actualization in compliance with the standards of legal and moral ethics of society
4. freedom, maintained by the choice to live crime-free.

These are the objectives and goals which the activities serve to build and enhance. Activities alone cannot meet these goals, any more than lectures alone can do so. Emotional expression and the process of sharing the expressed emotions are both required in order for the work to achieve its goals in the participants' lives.

Educational Corrections Declaration of Principles

As a sound basis for the orientation of any such program, the Correctional Education Association offers "A Declaration of Principles." These guiding thoughts were derived from the primary work of Thom Gehring, Carolyn R. Eggleston, and Stephen Duguid, and are premised on the need to infuse the wisdom of the humanities into correctional education.

Education is the process of discovering, acquiring, and developing individual skills, abilities and perspectives. Such a process of education may occur through teacher/peer, or student-centered instruction and learning. Correctional Education is the application of this process of education within correctional institutions and involves an appreciation of the special needs of prisoner-students, the special context of the school-in-prison, and the social dimension which society may impose on the educator. The Humanities comprise an approach to education that centers on a critical understanding of the relationship between human values, individual responsibility, and social context in determining both individual and group behavior.

This approach to Correctional Education sees the student as a complex actor in an equally complex social setting. Rejecting simplistic, single-issue "solutions" to the problem of crime, correctional educators stress individual responsibility and social context in helping students develop decision-making abilities, a critical understanding of self and society, and the ability and predisposition to exercise a wider range of options when faced with matters of choice. In this sense, correctional educators are change agents, using the humanities to help their students transform themselves into responsible, critical, and productive citizens.

In Correctional Education, the traditional education, focus on skills and knowledge is a luxury few can afford. Over-emphasis on content, in fact, may only produce "better-educated criminals" or "criminals with job skills," instead of fully functioning citizens. In our effort to improve correctional education, we are guided by tandem principles: citizenship, responsibility, and empowerment for students, and clarity and empowerment for educators. Toward these ends, we accept or reject the following according to their relevance to good correctional education practice:

Educational Techniques

We Accept These Strategies

• Cultural literacy and critical thinking skills can help students "think their way through life's problems" and are therefore equal in importance to the more fundamental and marketable skills.

• Professionalism, based on good practice and on research-supported literature.

• The empowerment of teachers and students and course content.

• Interrelated, humanities-based classroom activity.

• Conceiving of correctional education as a "core" program, with a focus on its role in the transforming the prison into a school.

We Reject These Strategies

• Reliance on superficial skill training, whether academic or vocational, which only tends to compartmentalize knowledge, avoiding ethical, controversial, or seemingly esoteric issues.

• Reliance on the "cult of the personality" and "good old boy" influence in setting priorities and solving problems.

- Coercion and manipulation of learners and the placing of student learning as a first priority.
- Correctional Educators as an integral part of prison management or as "window-dressing" for visitors and entertain-ment for prisoners.
- Technology as a substitute for classroom interaction.
- Correctional Education subject to non-educational priorities.

Organizational Structure

- Participatory management
- Integrity — consistency between long-term and short-term goals.
- National and international Correc-tional Education perspectives.
- Authoritarianism
- Opportunism — the sacrifice of long-term goals for short-term benefit.
- Isolation of Correctional Educators from others in the field.

Two Steps Forward, One Step Back

These goals are ideals to reach for. Regrettably, the educational system within WCCW has had budget cuts. Nevertheless, they are still creating much from very little, and forging ahead, pioneering new directions. Regrettably, pressure to ignore the ideology of "rehabilitation" has gradually eroded some of the progress that was made over the last thirty years. It has been replaced with a focus on confinement only. Fear-driven public sentiments are easy to stimulate, and the average citizen seems skeptical or uninterested in pursuing long-term solutions. But long-term solutions are essential to reverse the escalating trend of crime — crime as a social expression of personal discontent and estrangement from society.

Strategies to work against this social apathy remain in a nascent stage, where only a few Administrators and staff courageously allowed inmates to design, create, and implement programs that try out new alternatives. Volunteers who come in from outside the prison world have helped in empowering the inmates with new communication and interpersonal skills.

The View from WCCW's Education Department

I asked Larry Richardson about his concerns, and about what he has learned, as Director of Education at WCCW:

As a correctional/educational administrator, my hope is that this study catches the attention of legislators and those who dictate programs and allocate funds for WCCW.

Having taught and administered educational programs in both male and female institutions, I feel that there is a difference between men and women when considering recidivism. Women are generally seeking positive change; men, often, are not so motivated in pursuing self-change. My staff and I hope to assist by fueling each inmate's desire for self-advancement.

In seeking to reduce recidivism, individual needs must be part of the formula for success. Women at WCCW are in dire need of advanced education, vocational training, and spiritual-based and family-focused programs, and many need extended mental health treatment, and chemical dependency treatment. These are not "fluff" that can be cut when determining the needs for an institutional budget. Each woman's needs must be evaluated and addressed if we are to come up with the "proper mix" that will have a positive impact; treatment and program resources must be fully available if we are to be able to meet the different requirements of each inmate.

The issues that previously drove these women to substance abuse, dysfunctional relationships and economic strife were precursors to crime. These issues must be dealt with within prison, if we hope to keep these women from further criminal acts. With the majority of women testing out at an average of a sixth grade level, and with little or no history of maintaining a legal job, they are clearly not prepared to leave here and resume — or, rather, build from scratch — a normal life, with their children as dependants.

Education is a huge part of life success. Illustrating this, a recent study by the Correctional Educational Association (funded by the US Dept. of Education) found a definite correlation between recidivism and education (and library usage). Among this group of students and readers, recidivism was reduced by 27%.

Nevertheless, since 1996, resources allocated for education have decreased by as much as 10% per year. With staff reductions occurring at a time when population has increased, and with further decreases next year, I am more than concerned about the state of education here. Earning a GED is an accomplishment; however, outside of prison it does little but guarantee them a minimum-wage job (which currently traps the worker below poverty level). For that reason, offering a GED is not the ultimate goal for women here. To really make a dent in recidivism, we must offer real hope, by extending the education program with vocational training that promises a future for these women and their children. The GED should only be a stepping-stone for further advancement.

Programs aimed at boosting self-esteem and anger management should work hand in hand with vocational and educational skills. We do currently attempt to provide this, but resources are dwindling. Unfortunately, it is the male system that dominates program focus. The special needs and differences of women must be considered when designing programs.

I believe you can rehabilitate the female offender, if she first recognizes she "can" change her life. 80-90% of the women at WCCW are mothers. This presents a golden opportunity to use the prime motivator for change. These women need to be empowered, by positive female and male role models; they need to be taught everyday life skills such as parenting, responsibility, self-discipline, and budgeting in order to gain confidence that they can manage their lives in a meaningful and profound way. When less and less is offered, as our budgets are cut, these essential core programs cannot be available or lend themselves to these ends. This then perpetuates low self-esteem, and moves the women right back to their comfort zone. This normally consists of the very lifestyle that brought them here.

When inmates are motivated by fear of further failure, rather than a potential for success, change is difficult. As past president of the Washington State Education Association, my single goal was to communicate the correlation between success and the educational resources provided. If we implemented preventive measures and made an initial investment in people now, I believe we could save the State time and money while decreasing recidivism as well. Ultimately, this could save the State as much as $25,000 per year, per inmate, by not having them return.

Thoughts for the Future

Unquestionably, prison is not ideal. Make no mistake, the needs of women and their children in particular cannot be met very well under the current structure. The ideal would be legislative change to require a more objective approach from the very outset of a criminal investigation, so that when women are arrested, their histories as victims of abuse could be recognized. The process of classifying the degree and kind of culpability to assign to the woman should be conducted with this in mind, and sentencing should include the option of an alternative to our current prison environment.

A possible option could be a life skills community similar to the prison structure, mostly in that it would have a perimeter boundary maintained by correctional officers. The interior would be very different, in that families could stay long term within the prison, something like the way they do in conjugal visit stays; however, the family would also participate in the victim's awareness programs, AVP, church services, AA, NA, Peace Talks, parenting classes, and parent-child labs. To those who doubt that any such program could possibly find takers, I can say that I've spoken to many, many families that would rush to participate if the opportunity ever arose.

Education is valuable, but we must integrate our knowledge into demonstrated behavior, preparing relentlessly to create new responses, new attitudes that can become part of not just the female inmate's nature but that of her significant others. That cannot be accomplished by an "extended family visit" (EFV) for the few who can arrange it — and which "extends" for just over forty hours. The practice of life takes a great deal of living. Can our social awareness embrace the healthy family model for inmates and their families? Will we ultimately pay to hurt, or pay for communities to gain, in the end?

Employing prison-generated industries, gardens, farming, and production of products for distribution into the communities could provide real opportunities to practice the employable skills these women will need to survive legally in the world outside.

Lastly, tapping into the resources these women possess can offer the restorative justice so many have voiced their desire to be apart of.

Many programs have demonstrated their effectiveness, and there is an excruciating need to expand them. That, of course, requires will, volunteers, and funding — and it is the funding that is most lacking.

Some options are less costly than others. Without question, Peace Talks is a program that is operating successfully. For the women, the experience is extraordinary. The desire is there; the women at WCCW make it clear they want to participate in such work. They continually request longer and more frequent workshops; this is a positive opportunity, providing a real step in the right direction.

Another success for WCCW is the Girl Scouts Beyond Bars program. It's a unique arrangement implementing special accommodations to transport children who otherwise would be unable to visit their mothers in prison. This same transport service could be utilized in other programs that involve the parenting and victim awareness programs. The inclusion of the inmate's children presents a win-win solution to the restoring and the rebuilding of the necessary family bonds which, in turn, directly affect present and future criminal behavior.

Phone services are now available which provide an instant video-display of each party speaking on a phone line; access to this sort of privilege could be offered as an incentive for behavioral modification. Inmate Betterment Funds could purchase monthly access for mothers and their children.

Days not presently used for Extended Family Visits (conjugal visits) in the prison trailers can be made available for use, affording more opportunities for families to be together. The EFV program could be offered seven days a week — as it was in the past.

Female recidivism can be reduced through multi-disciplinary educational programs in our prisons. Specific suggestions, some of which have been implemented successfully at WCCW, include:

1. Classroom instruction on
    • victim awareness
    • parenting skills (parent-child labs)
    • communicational skills (assertiveness training, Toast Masters)
    • drug and alcohol treatment
    • defense mechanisms: what they are, and how to undo them
    • self-esteem building, and healthy relationships (family reunification)
    • nutrition and exercise

2. Peer-educating within units, addressing the above topics and offering mentoring.
    • Peer-educators should be on call for crisis conferencing (POCAAN offered this with their peer-educators)
    • Peer educators should be treated as and should see themselves as professionals. They should be trained and tested, paid wages, etc. (as in POCAAN)

3. Community-building and communication and social skills development through:
    • seminars
    • workshops
    • drama productions and role playing
    • poetry with raps and songs that focus on the identified issues
    • art expression and art shows (themes with the above topics)
    • outside guest speakers addressing the above issues (women's conference participants)
    • newsletter with questions and answers
    • prison channel broadcasting, videos and movies
    • outside family & friends' involvement in the presentations
    • games and contests to practice coping skills, such as solving a hypothetical dilemma (program staff provide a scenario and print it out for distribution; inmates together or individually can write solutions. With prizes to be given, and best answers posted in units).

4. Expanded Peace Talks programs. A secondary phase of this program could be "Bridging the GAP," wherein inmates who are four months short of leaving are involved in networking with community resources and get involved in the treatment plan.

5. The Rebuilding Families Organization. This could work with Bridging the Gap resources to provide additional community-based mentoring.

6. Job skills and work habits development in in-prison "businesses." With community and industry support, there could be opportunities in specific areas. To start the thinking, some ideas that come to mind are:
- contracts for secretarial work, computer work, drafting, landscape design
- clothing manufacturing or designing of products
- print shop, art work
- video production for educational TV: documentaries, creative arts

7. Grant writing — colleges and universities can be invited in to work with and mentor inmates.

The avenues to explore are too numerous to itemize and they are limited only by the resourcefulness of the present administrators and educators. Allowing a team of inmates to write letters and assist in creating these aforementioned projects are the type of activities that should be encouraged and guided. This would be self-actualizing and self-esteem building.

It's easy to say that these women don't deserve all that attention — so easy that one may forget that without it, not only they but their children will very likely be back as the involuntary wards of a society that doesn't care about what has been done to them, only what they have done.

When will we work together to stop these mothers from living in the ashes of society's broken dreams? If not now, then when? If not with your help, then with whose? To know a thing is to react to it. Silence, as they say, is complicity.

13. Conclusion

Toward an Incarceration that Rehabilitates

All of my experiences in this long stay in the prison system have made me consider many things that went beyond my crime. When I came to WCCW, I didn't know what had made me do what I did; really, I couldn't even comprehend anything more than the immediate reality of being where I was. My very first discovery came when another inmate (not a counselor, not a health worker, not a psychologist) actually helped me — drove me, really — to get off drugs.

When that happened, I was finally sane enough to realize what I had done; but still I had no idea why. I thought I was crazy and saw the whole prison as a kind of crazy-house where other women (who were not as mad as I was) were kept locked up just to keep them out of circulation. And, really, I thought at that time that it was a good thing — for them — because they were real criminals. I, of course, wasn't. Or so I thought.

The system, though, thought differently. I took it out by writing and painting, illustrating the politics of conditions in prison. My thoughts at that point weren't very coherent or pointed. I had too much past that I was carefully avoiding and too much present that often seemed as crazy as they said I was. One thing, though, slowly made its way deep into my consciousness. The other women were actually humans. They had plenty of flaws, but they were recognizably more like than unlike the people on the streets. As I slowly recovered from the cocaine madness, my natural sympathies led me in the direction of the programs covered in this book. As my fellow inmates became more distinctly human to me, through the clearing lens of my own humanity, I made the crucial discovery — it is fear, not craziness or "evil," that is at the root of most crime committed by women.

Once that was clear, the flaw in the system of imprisonment became clear also. More than any theory of punishment or incarceration, the ruling idea of imprisonment is intimidation. Prison exists to frighten the criminal into never attempting a crime again. It isn't just a loss of liberty; it is an enduring and unrelenting series of threats and graded punishments. A prisoner never lives in the secure feeling that she isn't in trouble; there's always something that can be — or can be made to *appear* to be — another infraction of the rules. Whether this is really the result of a conscious policy or just the consequence of a rather haphazard enforcement of a clumsy and ultimately futile attempt to secure perfectly conformist behavior, I don't know. It works as well or perhaps even better than if it were consciously done. Prison works, in the sense of inducing a mind-numbing perpetual fear, but that fails at its basic objective because it comes too late. Most of the women who come in have already experienced a whole lifetime of fear; this is just another chapter in it. They can't be scared off drugs; drugs are the only thing in their lives that get between them and the fear.

Realizing this, I could see how carefully one had to think about rehabilitation.

For the public, if a person comes out of prison and doesn't commit a crime, she's rehabilitated. It may be that by that point she is nothing more than a biologically functioning shell devoid of anything recognizable as humanity — numb, silent, cowed. To the public, at least, she's not committing crimes. Her shattered life doesn't count; after all, she did commit a crime and so, if this is the price, perhaps that will serve as a warning to others. The embarrassing fact, though, is that over the past forty years, in the face of escalating sentences and deteriorating conditions in prisons, the percentage of the population going to prison continues to rise. Someone's not getting the message.

The results of our work in WCCW suggest that there is another approach to the problem of crimes committed by women. Real rehabilitation is what would make the difference. Real rehabilitation would return a woman to society in a condition fit to participate, not just to exist somewhere in the shadows. Being fit to participate means a person who understands herself and how she came to crime, and how to support and live among other people.

The key to rehabilitation is not a huge, expensive social welfare program; it's using inmates to help inmates. No outsider can ever feel the inner pushes and strains that have led us to do as we do. Outsiders tend to apply theory to our lives precisely because they are so different from their own. Prisoners who help prisoners apply empathy; they have no need of theory to understand. Most of all, prisoners who help prisoners can at last feel dignity, the indispensable condition of freedom. They can cure crime, because they know from their own lives the forces that push us to crime. They cure themselves while setting others on the first steps toward cure. Just as the very best people at helping children with a problem are those children who have finally figured it out, so the best helpers to guide a woman on the first steps toward regaining her humanity are other women who have already gone a little farther up that path. It is time to stop thinking of all the women in prison as indistinguishably lost and criminal. It is time to stop the fear.

I propose a system of gradual emancipation of prisoners. A system that insists on responsibility for one's actions, not conformity. A system that actively recruits prisoners to help other prisoners. A system that builds trust and community among women rather than isolating them with the command to "just do your own time." A system that treats reintegration into the outside world as a gradual process which must begin inside the walls and continue for a long time. A system that treats lapses not as confirmation of uncontrollable criminality, but on the same scale as would be applied in the outside world. A system that looks for every evidence of socially useful humanity in the prisoner and seeks to encourage it. A system, above all, that pays full respect to that shining beacon in our society — the family.

The saddest and generally unnoticed victims of women's crimes are their children. Living among these women for so many years, the thing that stands out most in their sense of deprivation is not freedom, not love for some man, not love of material things; it is love for their children. Concern for her child, one or more, can be the most stabilizing or the most destructive force in a woman's life. Being cared for, even if inexpertly, by her mother is certainly the most stabilizing influence in the life of a child. The most hideous cruelty to children is not committed on the tiny infant who is capable of attachment to a substitute mother; it is the splintering of the bond between the mother and a child old enough to know the difference.

WCCW has recognized the value of mothering in a genuinely humane program which allows pregnant women who come to prison to bear and keep their children, but only if the mother will be released before the child is three. The policy recognizes the terrible pain inflicted on a child who is bonded to her mother when they are separated. But what happens to children whose mothers come to prison when the bond already exists?

To do something about that would require a much larger program, one that could only come about when public opinion finally begins to speak up on behalf of all those other children. I propose that in the future, prisons for women take on the responsibility of keeping all mothers and children together in all cases where there is not clear evidence of risk to the child. This would not automatically include situations of apparent neglect. Many mothers are as ignorant of how to be a mother as they are of their sexuality. Others, apparently neglectful, really simply were submerged in just trying to meet their bills, work obligations, and often the demands of a valueless and exploitative male. A positive environment with support and help from other women can turn these mothers into competent home makers, particularly when many of them have a blazing desire to provide better than the non-homes they came from.

This would amount to creating a colony within the prison, secure and genuinely productive. That, of course, raises another issue — work. Far from envisioning a sort of utopian place where women who have committed crimes now just spend their days being good mothers, the colony would have to accustom them not just to getting and holding a job, but to the grinding realities of juggling job and family — something their crimeless sisters on the outside know only too well. Shared responsibilities, carefully budgeted time and above all a hope to rise above minimum wage peonage would all be part of the system. The job skills women must learn go well beyond getting a poverty-wage job and then showing up every morning. It involves the unnoticed but foundational basis of the American dream — getting ahead. Millions of emigrants came to this country, recruited as low wage labor, but most of them found ways to move up in income and status. Any program that really aims to avoid recidivism, to prevent the destruction of families and the result that one generation after another sinks into poverty, crime and drugs, has to offer real hope. That means job skills beyond the impossibility of part-time, no-benefits, low-wage indigence.

The critical reader might at this point wonder whether, if all this were done, there might be so many desperate women outside the prison they would storm the place trying to get in. That leads to the next issue: feminism. The feminists have made great improvements in certain aspects of the lives of the middle class woman; now it's time for them to organize to help out their less successful sisters who have been left behind. That's going to be much more difficult. Class barriers, often in the form of distaste, are no respecters of gender, and even when the well-meaning middle class woman does break through, she often finds that the problems of poverty, abuse and despair seem insurmountable. That is where the successful graduates of the prison colony can be of invaluable help. If the women's organizations establish contacts and maintain them, the emerging ex-felon comes out into a world where pimps, abusers and exploiters won't be the only welcoming persons. These "graduates" will actually be bringing skills at living which they can share with other women who have never gone to prison; they will be peer educators, rather than a "slightly soiled" embarrassment to the outside world.

I'm not proposing another bureaucratically devised and administered program in which the people who run it see the whole thing in terms of their careers and the people in it think of it as pointless and over their heads. We need a form of cooperation between officialdom and volunteer organizations. To its credit, WCCW and other institutions have taken steps to make this happen, but the major impediment is still the idea of retributive justice. So long as prison exists primarily to make people suffer, no program, no matter how wise or successful will ever be tried if it defies that mandate. One of the major purposes of this writing is to try to make the public aware of the degree to which the woman offender, who has victimized someone else, so often has been a victim herself.

A Utopic System

A system to reduce female recidivism could conceivably be brought into existence with any prison system that generally resembles that of WCCW. This plan for reform could be called a "Life Skills Community Center."

Women are a separate class of people from men and this life skills center would address the specific needs of their class, the sorts of things they have identified in their own words. The central function of the Life Skills Community Center (LSC) would be to strengthen and/or develop the bonds of family, children and community. Research has shown that these are the areas which have the major impact on recidivism rates.

The LSC system would foster programs that bring in the outside families to participate in specific programs with the inmate resident. Parenting classes and Parent-Child Labs could integrate the entire family in learning the skill which would lead to success on the outside. Alternatives to Violence, Alcoholics Anonymous, Narcotics Anonymous and Substance Abuse Programs should be open to family members as well as inmates. If the family is the key to a successful rehabilitation, it's only sensible to take steps to ensure that it works positively rather than dragging the newly-freed inmate back down. Family dysfunction and lack of communication skills within the family are major problems, which the system must tackle to assure the departing inmate isn't in a revolving door. When a woman exits prison and attempts to employ the skills she learned in prison classes but is not reinforced with healthy life-affirming responses, she will return to her earlier patterns of denial or self-medication. If we can bridge the gap between sobriety within the prison and being substance free within the community, we can greatly improve her chances of successful reintegration in the free world.

WCCW has always been a national leader in what is termed the "model" prison movement. It is today one of only a very few to offer a program for family visits of two days' duration. These have been spectacularly successful in moderating inmate behavior as an incentive to behave well, and as a taste of real family life. Unfortunately, a male inmate in the Washington system murdered his wife, and that led to stringent rules which simply eliminated visits for any inmate, male or female, who was incarcerated for any sort of family-related violence.

This unfortunate application of the idea of equal opportunity or, really, equal disability, is a perfect example of false fairness. There is a great difference between a male who is in prison for a long history of violence against women and a woman who is there for having desperately responded to a life of savage abuse by resorting to deadly violence. Until some serious attention is paid to how these people actually lived before they came to prison, the road to rehabilitating women inmates will be full of ruts. Yet, it is exactly in the area of the relationship between men and women that the very core of the problem lies.

This study has shown how prevalent histories of abuse are for these women. They need opportunities to socialize with women and men who are healthy and uninvolved with crime. Recidivist rates and first time offender studies have shown that the mates these women have intimate relationships with are by and large involved in crime. Left to the chance encounters of bar and street corner, many of these women will easily fall victim to the same sort of partnership. The LSC would invite men and women with appropriate social and spiritual attitudes to participate in socials and educational workshops. At least, the women will gain a different point of reference, a broader standard.

Presently, many women in prison put their names and photos on the Internet Babes Behind Bars mating service. It's easy for free world people to dismiss this as a shoddy imitation of a mail order bride situation, in which both parties exaggerate their advantages and take a chance on what they will get. The truth is worse. These women often have never known a non-abusive relationship or a man who isn't a criminal. Leaving prison, they feel the stigma of being a convict and this makes them think they are only fit for the troublesome partner they will shortly meet. I can't count how many women have told me they don't know how to talk to nice men, or woman, or where to meet them. Creating opportunities to form relationships based on honesty and substance-free relationships can only serve the best interest, not merely of the woman and her children, but of society as well. Incarceration costs at least $25,000 per year. Calculating an average term of five years, plus court costs, the price of their social failure is $125,000. Recidivism is expensive to more than the offender. Our government simply needs to recognize the factors that make for crime or not-crime, and pay the smaller cost for the better outcome. To do that, we will have to open the prison doors and let the community in.

The lives of children here, now, or in foster care, or those yet to be born, are a real responsibility for all of us. If we continue to make the most minimal provision in the belief that their mothers are genuinely "bad," we set their feet on the same path that led their mothers into prison. They will be the victims of tomorrow and your children will walk beside them.

Women are not men; we need not fear them as much as we do the "rogue" male. Women do not need to be taught not to be violent; they need understanding, support, education in goal setting, life skills and relationships, and opportunity.

As women pass through the LSC system, there should be further options. Early partial release through the use of home monitoring devices could be a major help in reducing prison crowding, the costs of incarceration and the shock of stepping out the door. The LSC program should be seen as an experimental effort, to find out what works and what does not. I envision, over the longer haul, a system in which there is something like the underground railway that once helped slaves escape to freedom. This one, though, should be more like a monorail, something so visible it can't be missed. I hope to live to see the day when graduates of the colony leave prison secure in the knowledge that their sisters who left earlier are on hand to help; that there is support from women's organizations who, knowing neighborhoods, knowing people, can help with finding decent living quarters, in finding a decent job. Who help most of all simply by being there — something so necessary for the emotional health of a woman.

I want to give credit to the brave and humane people who put these policies in place at WCCW; often in the face of official DOC attitudes. If they had not taken the chance they did, when they let the first of us into SNU, into TEC, to facilitate for POCAAN and AVP, and now Peace Talks, we would never have known how much could be done. And they would never have known how many of us wanted to do something. And in recognizing the humanity of these women and men, ranging from Correctional Officers all the way up to the very Superintendent's office, I realize that government agencies have a great role to play in my monorail. We need each other.

All of this sounds awfully utopian, I know. It hasn't got a lot of specifics and it seems to say that women are special creatures who somehow get pushed into criminal lives and are only waiting for a chance to be better. To the critic who smiles at my naiveté, I only can respond that real reform only comes from a combination of two things — a dream, and a willingness to find real ways to accomplish it. We found some of them when we dared to dream that mere felons could actually help one another. We were right. Those who catch hold of this dream will have to find their own ways. Not every effort will succeed, but every failure is something valuable learned; every refusal to try is a final failure with nothing learned. Abolitionists were once a tiny band, despised as impractical dreamers and fanatics. One day their dream became such a reality that now no one can imagine going back to what was there before. I see prison reform as another kind of emancipation, one which will begin with the woman felon but eventually extend to her sisters struggling with histories of abuse, neglect and poverty. We know now that those things are not natural and irreversible any more than slavery was. I hope this book will be a small station on the monorail of the liberation of women from trauma, abuse, exploitation and despair.

> "What would help me? Well, people who truly care about what happens to me and what my future holds. More people who can relate in some way, better law actions. They need to do better background checks or scan, help people who need emotional, physical and mental therapy. Help those who need rehabilitation whether it is for drugs or any other addictions or physical and mental problems. Programs for women who have children after the prison gates especially for women who have long term prison sentences and need a whole new start at life." (H7)

Let us therefore follow after the things which make for peace, and things wherewith one may edify another.
Romans 14:19

Appendices

Population at Washington Corrections Center for Women
Increase of "New Commitments"

In an interview in April 2001, the WCCW Records Manager noted that new "commitments" have steadily risen. From 1990 to 1997, the average female admissions were 400 per year, but they gradually rose over that eight-year period to about 480 admissions per year. Then, admissions jumped 25% in 1998-1999, and again from 1999 to spring 2001, and another 25% by September 2002. The current population count is over 900, exceeding the maximum capacity of the prison.

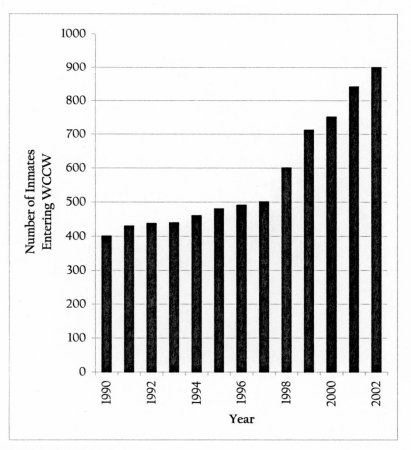

Source: WCCW Records Manager

If recent incarceration rates remain unchanged, an average of 1 out of every 20 persons (5.1%) will serve time in prison during his or her lifetime, according to Department of Justice Bureau of Justice Statistics reports (February 9, 2001).

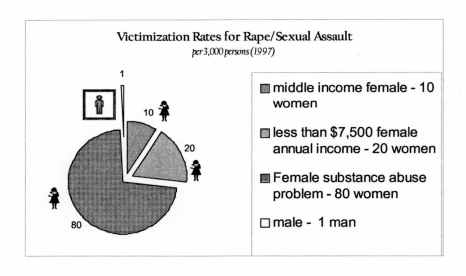

Prisoners Male and Female 1980 to 1999
Under the Jurisdiction* of Federal and State Authorities
(Rather than those in Custody)

[Based on U.S. Census Bureau - Bureau Of Justice Statistics Estimated Resident Population,
As of December 31, 2001]

*Probation, Jail, Prison (State and Federal), Parole: Totals combined 5,057,050 (Females: 951,918)
1998 sources: Beck, A.J. (2000) Prison and Jail Inmates at mid-year 1999. Beck, A.J. and Mumola, C.J. (1999).
Prisoners in 1998. Bonczar, T.P. and Glaze, (1999) Probation and Parole.

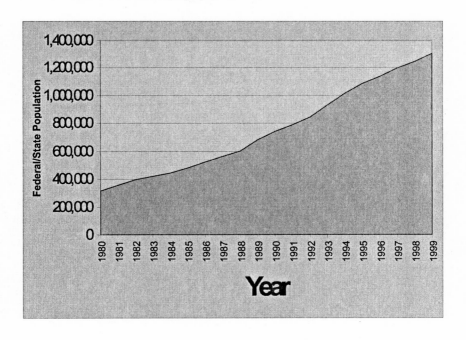

Prisoners Male and Female 1980 to 1999
Under the Jurisdiction* of Federal and State Authorities
(Rather than those in Custody)

1980	315,974
1981	353,673
1982	395,516
1983	419,346
1984	443,398
1985	480,568
1986	522,084
1987	560,812
1988	603,732
1989	680,907
1990	739,980
1991	789,610
1992	846,277
1993	932,074
1994	1,016,691
1995	1,085,022
1996	1,137,722
1997	1,195,498
1998	1,245,402
1999	1,305,393

Increase of Women Inmates (Federal/State Facilities)
1980-1999 (as of December 31, 1999)

A 7-times increase over 20 years!
This leap illustrates the importance of addressing female-offender issues.

By the end of 1998, almost one million women were under some form of correctional supervision.
Since 1990, the female prisoner population has nearly doubled (92%): men increased only by 67%.
The annual rate of growth on incarcerated women (8.4) has surpassed men (males 6.5) (Beck and Mumola 1999)

1980	12,331
1981	14,298
1982	16,441
1983	17,476
1984	19,205
1985	21,345
1986	24,544
1987	26,822
1988	30,145
1989	37,264
1990	40,564
1991	43,802
1992	46,501
1993	54,037
1994	60,125
1995	63,963
1996	69,599
1997	73,835
1998	77,600
1999	82,594

*Based on U.S. Census Bureau, Statistical Abstract of the United States, 2001

THEORETICAL MODEL
FOR PATTERNS IN SURVIVAL/ATTEMPTS TO COPE WITH ABUSE
(PHYSICAL, SEXUAL, PSYCHOLOGICAL)

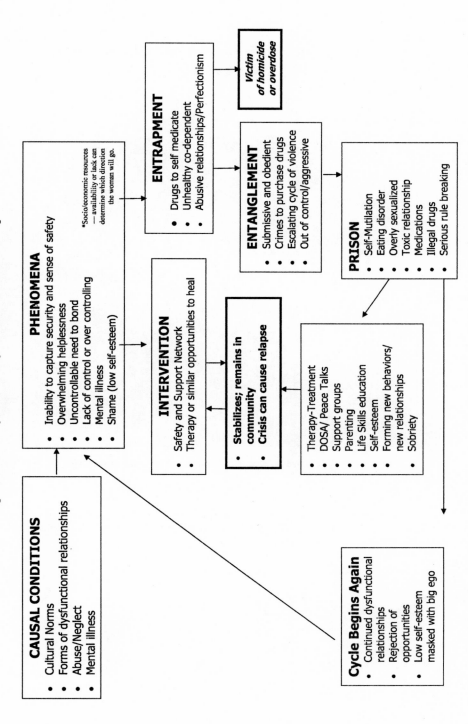

CAUSAL CONDITIONS
- Cultural Norms
- Forms of dysfunctional relationships
- Abuse/Neglect
- Mental illness

PHENOMENA
- Inability to capture security and sense of safety
- Overwhelming helplessness
- Uncontrollable need to bond
- Lack of control or over controlling
- Mental illness
- Shame (low self-esteem)

*Socio/economic resources — availability or lack can determine which direction the woman will go.

ENTRAPMENT
- Drugs to self medicate
- Unhealthy co-dependent
- Abusive relationships/Perfectionism

Victim of homicide or overdose

ENTANGLEMENT
- Submissive and obedient
- Crimes to purchase drugs
- Escalating cycle of violence
- Out of control/aggressive

PRISON
- Self-Mutilation
- Eating disorder
- Overly sexualized
- Toxic relationship
- Medications
- Illegal drugs
- Serious rule breaking

INTERVENTION
- Safety and Support Network
- Therapy or similar opportunities to heal

Stabilizes; remains in community
Crisis can cause relapse

- Therapy-Treatment
- DOSA/ Peace Talks
- Support groups
- Parenting
- Life Skills education
- Self-esteem
- Forming new behaviors/ new relationships
- Sobriety

Cycle Begins Again
- Continued dysfunctional relationships
- Rejection of opportunities
- Low self-esteem masked with big ego

Drug and/or Alcohol Abuse and Sexual/Physical Abuse
Rates of Women

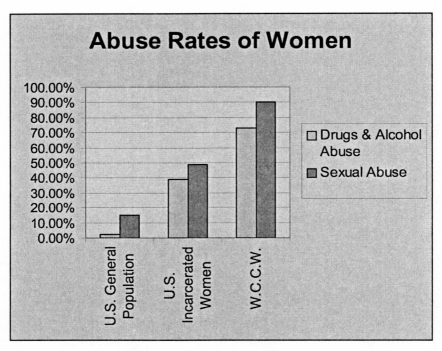

- U.S. and Canada Sexual abuse of children estimates: 20%-45% women (Geffner, 1992; Wyatt and New Comb, 1990)
- Addicts are involved in approximately three to five times as many crimes as non-addicts (Fletcher et.al., 1993, p.49)
- (Harlow, 1999) Incarcerated (Gorey and Leslier, 1997) general population
- (Wallace, 2001) WCCW *note 12% of respondents refuse to answer the question of substance abuse history.

LIFE UNDER THE WASHINGTON STATE DEPARTMENT OF CORRECTIONS (DOC)

A. Inmate Costs and Earning Opportunities

Most women at WCCW work for the institution in the following categories.

- Kitchen worker
- Janitorial
- Groundskeeper
- Maintenance
- Laundry
- Educational tutors - data processing - clerical

The maximum pay they can earn is $55.00 per month, whether they work 6 hours per day or 9. From this $55.00 monthly income, each woman must purchase all her own hygiene needs, soap, shampoo, toothpaste, deodorant, lotion, tampons, and coffee, etc. Additionally, she must buy her own clamp lamp and bulbs, TV, or radio. Buying from the canteen, women pay 15% more than a consumer in the community. All money sent in from friends and family has 35% deducted, so a $100 gift becomes $65 which has $55.25 in purchasing power. (A percentage of the deductions go to a victims' fund, and an enforced savings program.)

Telephone calls must be made "collect" and are assessed steep processing fees. A local 12-minute call to a home five miles away costs about $6. A call 60 miles away goes up to about $13. This imposes a financial burden on families that accept the call. For most mothers in WCCW, these costs preclude any telephone communication with their children or at the very least put a severe limit on their contact. Because women are relationship-oriented, these financial burdens often create conflicts over family resources. For some, the mothers adapt by using discarded paper and cardboard to create toys and gifts for their children really, nothing goes unsalvaged. Once a gift for a loved one is made, the woman must then sacrifice from her little money in order to cover the cost of mailing the item. Only the highest delivery rates are offered —first class mail, or UPS. Still, with such limits on her money, it is very common to see an inmate share what little she has with others who have less. Risking infractions and punishment, women as a rule will freely give a bar of soap, a cigarette, a cup of coffee, or a snack, rather than see another woman go without. Unfortunately, because some male inmates strong-arm, steal or take from weaker inmates, a state rule was made prohibiting all acts of sharing or gifting other inmates. This rule may be needed for men, but for women it sacrifices the spirit of compassion and empathy. It is extremely rare for one woman to strong-arm another — manipulation is more likely where one woman promises to repay another but never does.

B. Rules and Social Policies

Clothing packages may be sent in to the facility four times a year, but much of an inmate's package can be rejected. Restrictions include:

- No black, dark/medium blue, burgundy, forest green, deep purple, or gray
- Shoes cannot have any metal eyelets, shanks
- Clothing must be labeled "machine wash and dry"
- Allowed: 3 tops, 3 bottoms, and 2 pairs of shoes
- No more than 4 pockets

Restrictions on contact with children and visitors is one of the most painful deprivations for mothers. One 2-second hug and a kiss before the visit and one when the visitor leaves are all that is allowed until the child reaches the age of ten. Then, only hand-holding contact is permitted. Complaints are constant: "I brushed a strand of hair off my 15-year-old's forehead and got in trouble," "My mom put her hand on my shoulder while talking," "My daughter was crying and I wiped a tear from her cheek," "My son gave me a second hug before he left." All these are infractable behaviors. Many ask if this stringent level of restriction is too excessive and unnecessary, only further distancing already strained relationships rather than encouraging family bonding.

In behaviors other than visiting, inmates can be infracted for pro-social behaviors like shows of empathy, saving leftover food, feeding the birds, using the wrong toilet area, grooming another women's hair (braiding or trimming), sharing clothes or talking at another women's cell doorway.

WCCW is not a typical prison environment. It is struggling to achieve the best it can within tight constraints. There is unusual humanity and, at the same time, there are those tendencies toward petty-mindedness. Infractions can be excessive to the point of the ridiculous. On the positive side, that does provide safety and security for the prisoner. There are almost never serious fights, nor is there any great drug trafficking. Few drugs get in and crime is almost nonexistent. (One woman may steal another's jeans or cosmetics from her cell.)

Unfortunately, most the basic nature is to nurture (even if it is not politically correct to say so). Shows of affection and sometimes romantic love between the women are forcefully restricted, by moving one to another living unit, punishing even non-sexual displays of affection (as though they were sexual) and so on. Sexual activity is prohibited, and is nipped well before it can bud. Much of the affection between these women represents nothing more than a basic female need to express tenderness and create relationships that provide safety and nurturing. Naturally, there are those who use and abuse a woman's affections, replicating the abusive roles these women often have experienced in the community. Petty jealousies, rivalries, and infidelities create the biggest problems and prove a disservice and misrepresentation to those genuinely love-based and healing relationships. Rape is also nearly non-existent.

C. The Prison Charities

Some outstanding prison community work is seen in the Arts and Crafts programs. Here, women come to make charity gifts for the community outside. Ceramics are made for local soup lines, blankets are made for AIDS babies and the homeless, toys are made for battered women's shelters, and many other causes are served.

Quarterly food sales are offered as fundraisers. A markup is made to raise money for non-profit groups in the community, with a primary focus on groups who help children, and battered women shelters.

To help make these things happen, staff members generously work overtime, without pay.

These and other activities allow the prisoners to give back to the community. Some of the inmates work tirelessly to make these programs successful and often their enormous contributions are unknown by the community. It should be noted that not one of these activities could occur without the staff assisting.

Another unknown charity group operating in the prison is comprised of volunteers and WCCW staff. Gifts are purchased and then donated to the Christmas gift fund. Each year, mothers are allowed a special day to celebrate with their children. The donated gifts are chosen by the mother to give as presents to their children.

D. Population Increase at WCCW

In an interview in April 2001, the WCCW Records Manager noted that new "commitments" have steadily risen. From 1990 to 1997, the average female admissions were 400 per year, but they gradually rose over that eight-year period to about 480. Then, admissions jumped 25% in 1998-1999, and again from

1999 to spring 2001, and another 25% by September 2002. The current population count is over 900, exceeding the maximum capacity of the prison.

If recent incarceration rates remain unchanged, an average of 1 out of every 20 persons (5.1%) will serve time in prison during his or her lifetime, according to Department of Justice Bureau of Justice Statistics reports (February 9, 2001).

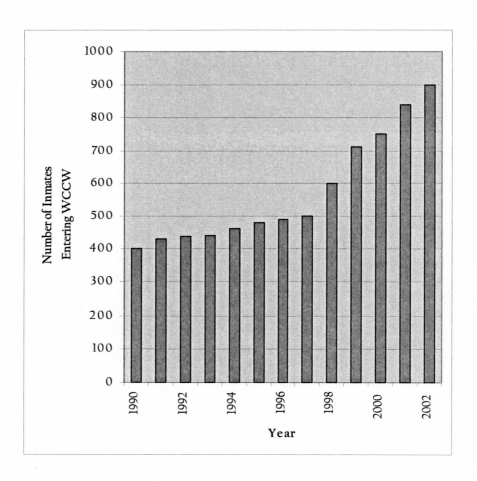

Source: WCCW Records Manager

RESOURCES

Books

Belknap, Joanne (1996) *Invisible Woman — Gender, Crime, & Justice.* Wadsworth Publishing.

Covington, Stephanie, and Liana Beckett (1988) *Leaving the Enchanted Forest— The Path from Relationship Addiction to Intimacy.*

Covington, Stephanie (1991) *Awakening Your Sexuality: A Guide for Recovering Women.*

Maltz, Wendy (1991) *The Sexual Healing Journey: A Guide for Survivors of Sexual Abuse.*

Maltz, Wendy and Beverly Holman (1987) *Incest and Sexuality: A Guide to Understanding and Healing.*

Mellody, Pia, Andrea Wells Miller, Keith J. Miller (1989) *Facing Co-Dependence: What It Is, Where It Comes From, How It Sabotages Our Lives.*

Nichoff, Debra (1999) *The Biology of Violence: How Understanding the Brain, Behavior and Environment Can Break the Vicious Circle of Aggression.*

Owen, Barbara (1998) *In the Mix: Struggle and Survival in a Women's Prison.* Albany, NY: State University of New York Press.

Palmer, Cynthia, and Michael Horowitz (2000) *Sisters of the Extreme: Women Writing on The Drug Experience.*

Pert, Candace B. and Deepak Chopra (1997) *Molecules of Emotion: Why You Feel the Way You Feel.*

Restak, Richard (2000) *The Secret Life of the Brain.*

Authorities on Topics of Specific Relevance

Asch, S.E. (e.g., opinions and social pressure)

Asch, S.E. (forming impressions of personality)

Aserinsky, E., & Kleitman, N. (phenomena during sleep)

Bandera, A., Ross, D., Ross, S.A. (e.g., transmission of aggression through imitation of aggressive models)

Calhoun, J.B. (e.g., population density and social pathology)

Darley, J.M., & Latane, B. (bystander intervention in emergencies: diffusion of responsibility)

Dement, W., Cartwright, R.D., Hobson, J.A. & McClearly, R.W., (dream theory)

Ekman, P., & Friesen, W.V. (constants across cultures in the face and in emotions)

Festinger, L., & Carlsmith, J.M. (e.g., cognitive consequences of forced compliance)

Freud, A. (e.g., the ego and mechanisms of defense)

Friedman, M., & Rosenman, R.H. (association of specific overt behavior pattern with blood and cardiovascular findings)

Gazzaniga, M.S. (split-brain)

Gibson, E.J., & Walk, R.D. (The Visual Cliff)

Harlow, H.F. (e.g., nature of love)

Herman, J. (e.g., trauma and recovery)

Holmes, T.H., & Rahne, R.H. (e.g., the social re-adjustment rating scale)

Kohlberg, L. (development of children's orientations toward a moral order sequence in the development of moral thought)

Langer, E.J., & Rodin, J., (e.g., effects of choice and enhanced personality for the aged: field experiment in an institutional setting)

LaPiere, R.T. (e.g., attitudes and actions)

Loftus, E.R. (e.g., leading questions and the eye witness report)

Masters, W.H., & Johnson, V.E. (e.g., human sexual response)

Milgram, S. (e.g., behavioral study of obedience)

Miller, D. (e.g., trauma re-enactment syndrome).

Murray, H.A. (e.g., explorations in personality)

Pavlov, I.P. (e.g., conditioned reflexes)

Piaget, J. (e.g., development of object concept. Zajonc, R.B., & Markus, G.B. (birth order and intellectual development)

Rorschach, H. (e.g., psychodiagnostics: a diagnostic test based on perception)

Rosenhan, D.L. (e.g., being sane in insane places)

Rosenthal, R., & Jacobson, L. (teacher's expectations/I.Q. gains)

Rosenzweig, M.R., Bennett, E.L., & Diamond, M.C. (brain changes in response to experience)

Rotter, J.B. (e.g., generalized expectancies for internal vs. external control of reinforcement)

Seligman, M.E.P., & Maier, S.F. (failure to escape traumatic shock)

Skinner, B.F. (e.g., superstition in pigeons)

Smith, M.L., & Glass, G.V. (e.g., meta-analysis of psychotherapy outcome studies)

Spanos, N.P. (e.g., hypnosis)

Terr, L. (memories)

Tolman, E.C. (cognitive maps in rats and men)

Turnbull, C.M. (BaMuti Pygmies)

Walker, L. (battered women pathology)

Watson, J.B. & Rayner, R. (e.g., conditioned emotional responses)

Whitehead, W.E., Blackwell, B., & Robinson, A. (e.g., effects of diazepam on phobic avoidance behavior and phobic anxiety)

Wolfe, J. (e.g., the systematic desensitization treatment of neuroses)

Other works on the importance of choice and the perception of having control include:

Boschen, K. 1996). Correlates of life satisfaction, residential satisfaction, and locus of control among adults with spinal cord injuries. *Rehabilitation Counseling Bulletin,* 394), 230-243.

Cornwell, Y., Pearson, J., & Derenzo, E. 1996). Indirect self-destructive behavior among elderly patients in nursing homes: A research agenda. *American Journal of Geriatric Psychiatry,* 4 2), 152-163.

Draper, P. 1996). Compromise, massive encouragement, and forcing: a discussion on the mechanisms used to limit the choices available to the older adult in-hospital. *Journal of Clinical Nursing,* 55), 325-331.

Hall, B., & Bocksnick, J. 1996). Therapeutic recreation for the institutionalized elderly: Choice of abuse? *Journal of Elder Abuse and Neglect,* 74), 49-60.

Rodin, J. 1986). Aging and health: Effects of the sense of control. *Science,* 233, 1271-1276.

Rodin, J., & Langer, E.J. 1977). Long-term effects of a control relevant intervention with the institutionalized aged. *Journal of Personality and Social Psychology*, 35, 897-902.

Rodin, J., Soloman, S., & Metcalf, J. 1979). Role of control in mediating perceptions of density. *Journal of Personality and Social Psychology*, 36, 988-999.

Schulz, R. 1976). Effects of control and predictability on the psychological well-being of the institutionalized aged. *Journal of Personality and Social Psychology*, 33, 563-573.

Taylor, S.E., et al: "Female Responses to Stress: Tend and Befriend, Not Fight or Flight." *Psychological Review*, (2000) 107, (3), PP.41-429.

Williams, S., & Luthan, F. 1992). The impact of choice of rewards and feed back on task performance. *Journal of Organizational Behavior*, 13, 653-666.

ACKNOWLEDGEMENTS

The author wishes to thank Dr. James Wallace for his critical eye and his assistance in keeping her on track, for believing in her and encouraging her to bring this study to completion; and Eliz Johnson, for serving as liaison with her publisher and for putting the materials on disk.

Special thanks to Larry Richardson, a mentor and pioneer for special projects at WCCW, who guided the study.

For their patience and love, the author thanks her children, Steve and Juliette, who sacrificed time with their mother so that she could do this work.

Jennifer Furio, author of numerous books, is a special friend and sister in the struggle to bring to the public information about women in prison and the promise of restorative justice. The author is grateful for her inspiration and love.

Much gratitude is extended to the following Washington State Department of Corrections staff: Superintendent James Walker, Superintendent Belinda Stewart, Superintendent Alice Payne (CPM), Dr. Michael Robbins, Director of Washington State Mental Health Services for the Department of Corrections, Lieutenant Gerald Isham, Sergeant Rod Coberly.

Credit is due to Dr. Angela Wade, whose work at WCCW transformed the lives of her Survivors of Sexual Abuse (SOSA) group, and to Debi Acey, my friend and text appraiser who assisted me in preparing the final stages of this manuscript. Others whose work at WCCW contributed to this study include Peace Talks WCCW liaison and lead facilitator Charlotte Carroll, and past facilitators of the Alternatives to Violence Janet Haynes and DeAnna Martin.

Lastly, to the innovative and remarkable professors at Evergreen State College, particularly Kate Crowe and Mark Hurst, who supported this study for PLE credit; and to my editor Andrea Secara, who saw potential and listened to the voices of the women in this book, their message and their need to be heard. Thank you for your help and talent in this project.

All author's profits will be donated to the Kitsap Sexual Assault Center/ Rape Response in Port Orchard, WA, and the Rebuilding Families Program, WCCW, at the author's request.

Printed in the United States
1165000001B/41

9 780875 861654